Contents

Acknowledgements

The author and publisher are grateful to the following for permission to reproduce materials:

Ann and Bury Peerless Slide Resources and Picture Library, cover (bottom left) ● Barry Swain, pages 3, 10, 64 ● Eluned Cole, pages 38 (right), 39, cover (bottom right) ● Harjinder S. Sagoo, pages 1, 13, 15, 19, 21, 36, 38 (left), 44, 47, 50, 61, 71, 79, 85 (top), 93, 99 ● J. Kalidas, page 16 ● W. Owen Cole, pages 2, 9, 22, 33, 42, 49, 52, 60, 66, 69, 85 (bottom), 90 (top), 92 (left) amd cover (top left)● Sally and Richard Greenhill, cover (top right) ● Sikh Information Centre, Leeds, pages 27, 40, 56, 76, 82, 90 (bottom), 96.

Every effort has been made to contact copyright holders and we apologise if any have been overlooked.

The cover photographs show:

(top left) *Kar seva* at the Golden Temple – the ceremonial removal of silt from the bed of the lake (*sarowar*) undertaken every 50 years; (top right) a British Sikh policeman; (bottom left) young Sikhs representing two sons of Guru Gobind Singh at a Sikh festival in India; (bottom right) Sikhs representing the *panj pyare* at the Baisakhi procession in Southall, London.

WORLD RELIGIONS SERIES
Series Editor: W. Owen Cole

Sikhism

Piara Singh Sambhi

Stanley Thornes & Hulton

Much of the manuscript of this book was typed by Hilary Yeld shortly before her last illness. She worked at Bishop Otter College for 15 years and is greatly missed by her former colleagues. This book is dedicated to her memory with respect and affection as a small token of friendship.

Text © Piara Singh Sambhi 1989
Original line illustrations © Stanley Thornes (Publishers) Ltd 1989

First published in 1989 by:
Stanley Thornes (Publishers) Ltd
Ellenborough House
Wellington Street
CHELTENHAM GL50 1YD
England

Reprinted 1994

British Library Cataloguing in Publication Data

Sambhi, Piara Singh
   Sikhism.
   1. Sikhism
   I. Title   II. Series
   294.6

   ISBN 1-871402-12-3

Typeset by Tech-Set, Gateshead, Tyne & Wear
Printed and bound in Great Britain at Redwood Books, Trowbridge, Wiltshire

Chapter 1

Introduction

Sikhism is one of the youngest of the world's religions. It is numerically small but well known worldwide.

> The Sikhs are a dynamic and versatile community. They are seen in practically every walk of Indian life. Wherever there are Indians there must be Sikhs. In the military and the universities, in business, trade and practically all aspects of Indian life, Sikh influence seems to be predominant. There are only about 12 million or so in a country of over 650 million, yet it seems that they wield power and influence far out of proportion to their numbers.
>
> D. P. Singhal, *A History of the Indian People* (Methuen, 1983)

> Sikhs have a distinctly martial mien and tradition. They are the most distinctive of India's minorities. They are proud, enterprising, assertive, pragmatic. Not too privately, they consider themselves a cut above the rest and there is some justification in their swagger.
>
> Trevor Fishlock, *India File* (John Murray, 1983)

These statements from a distinguished Indian historian and a British journalist highlight the best-known traits of the Sikh community. More than 80 per cent of the world Sikh population still live in the small north Indian state of the Punjab and the neighbouring areas of Haryana and Delhi. Outside India, the United Kingdom has the largest Sikh community, numbering over a third of a million Sikhs, followed by Canada, USA, East Africa, and Singapore. Most of them still have links with the Punjab.

Children learning Punjabi in a British gurdwara *(the Sikh place of worship).*

Reading the Sikh scripture, called the Guru Granth Sahib.

1   **a** Find out where the Punjab is on a map of India.
    b Try to discover something about its climate and the crops which are grown there.
2   Prepare a world map so that you can mark on it the countries mentioned in this book where Sikhs have settled.

Sikhs believe in one God. Their places of worship and the social institutions which they provide, such as schools and colleges, hospitals and orphanages, are open to all. Sikh worship consists of listening to, reciting and singing the praises of God. Anyone may join in the service. The Sikh scriptures contain the revelations of men of God from various castes and creeds, along with those of the Sikh Gurus. Sikhism does not, therefore, claim the exclusive monopoly of truth and accepts the validity and coexistence of other faiths. But if the beliefs and practices of a faith are not amenable to reason, if its doctrines come into conflict with known facts, or impinge upon the natural rights of human equality and brotherhood, then a Sikh will not hesitate to criticise it. Sikhism is no longer a missionary religion; it is persuasive but not coercive.

No one who is indifferent to the sufferings of others is really spiritual, hence the Sikh emphasis on the selfless service of others. To be a Sikh today is to share the teachings of the Sikh Gurus, attempt to be faithful to them and put them into practice in the everyday world.

What is the difference between a religion or political system being persuasive and being coercive?

Chapter 2

The Sikh Gurus

GURU NANAK (1469–1539)

The story of Sikhism begins with the teachings of Guru Nanak. He was born in 1469 in a middle-class Hindu family of fairly good village standing. His father, Kalyan Das, kept the revenue accounts of a feudal landlord, Rai Bular, a Muslim convert from Hinduism. Guru Nanak's birthplace, the village of Talwandi, is about 65 kilometres to the south-west of Lahore in Pakistan. It is now known as Nankana Sahib in honour of the founder of Sikhism. His parents gave him a good education and he worked for about 14 years as a storekeeper for the provincial governor, Nawab Daulat Khan Lodhi, at Sultanpur. His intensely religious bent of mind, however, was never at peace with wealth and status. He longed to serve the people and to work for their spiritual and moral welfare.

At the time of Guru Nanak, Muslim rule was firmly established in the major part of north India and the Hindus and Muslims had completely separated themselves from one another, religiously and socially.

What impression of Guru Nanak do you think the artist was trying to give in this portrait of him?

Guru Nanak advocated the worship of one God. He stressed the importance of collective worship in addition to individual private prayers. Meditating on the name of God and singing God's praises were the mode of worship. Women were welcomed to the congregations and encouraged to join fully in the religious and social activities of the community. Worship was to be offered in the spoken language of the people, Punjabi, and could be led by anyone regardless of their sex and status. The sharing of a meal, sitting together after the act of worship, was insisted upon to promote unity and to break the caste barriers (see Chapter 17) on eating together. Guru Nanak pointed out that God was within every individual and could be reached through worship, selfless service of fellow human beings, earning an honest living and helping the needy with money and material goods. These were some of the teachings which were further developed by the Gurus according to the time and circumstances.

?

How might meal sharing promote unity and break down barriers?

The First Congregations

Most of Guru Nanak's middle years were spent in missionary journeys in India and the adjoining countries to the north-west. At many places, *sangats* (congregations) were established in response to his new message. In later life he settled with his family at Kartarpur, a village founded by him on the bank of the River Ravi. People from far and near came there on pilgrimage and the place grew in size and importance. The visitors shared a disciplined life and simple worship with the residents, who welcomed them to the house of the Guru and made their stay comfortable. They meditated on God in the early morning and late in the evening, joined in the congregational singing of hymns composed by Guru Nanak, and listened to Guru Nanak's sermons, which covered a wide range of the religious and moral questions of the day. Some wrote down whatever they heard from the Guru or others about his travels; some prepared copies of the hymns of the Guru for the use of the scattered congregations. Others cooked and distributed food to one and all from the common kitchen, taking pleasure in washing up and keeping the place neat and tidy.

One of the people who visited Kartarpur was Bhai Lehna, a worshipper of Durga (a Hindu deity) from the nearby village of Khadur. He found himself so overwhelmed by the spiritual atmosphere of Kartarpur that he became a disciple of Guru Nanak on meeting him for the very first time. His devotion to the Guru and commitment to his ideals soon won him the title Angad (my limb) from Guru Nanak. A few years later, just before Guru Nanak himself died, he nominated Angad to be his successor and carry on the mission which he had begun.

?

1   Why do you think Guru Nanak decided to choose a successor rather than leave it to the community after his death?
2   What qualities would Guru Nanak be looking for in his successor?

GURU ANGAD (1539–52)

Guru Nanak had prepared the soil and planted the tree of Sikhism. Guru Angad's role was to ensure its growth and to give it a distinct shape and character.

Gurmukhi

Guru Angad is credited with the invention and popularisation of Gurmukhi, the script in which the Sikh scriptures are written. Sanskrit was the religious language of the Hindus and they used Devanagari script for writing it. For everyday matters, Punjabis used Lande (which means 'clipped'), a rough and crude type of script.

Lande was also used extensively by the mercantile classes for keeping accounts, and Guru Angad himself was a petty trader. He improved and perfected the Lande script on the lines of the Devanagri alphabet and used it for writing down the *Bani* (revelations) of Guru Nanak. The new script came to be called Gurmukhi, meaning that it came from the mouth of the Guru.

Guru Angad opened a school at Khadur and found time to give lessons to children in Gurmukhi. He urged his followers to learn the new script and teach it to others. It was a calculated step to wean away the Sikhs from Hinduism and to break the monopoly of brahmins, the Hindu priestly caste, over the world of learning.

Hymns and Teachings

We have only a small number of hymns from Guru Angad, but he used the name 'Nanak' in the concluding line of each of them, indicating that he was one in spirit and essence with his master, Guru Nanak. All the succeeding Gurus followed this convention to emphasise the continuity and oneness of the message.

Guru Angad emphasised the importance of household life and of physical fitness, especially through wrestling exercises and other sports. This had a particular significance at the time. Sri Chand, the elder son of Guru Nanak, had renounced the world, and had a sizeable following of disciples who practised celibacy and asceticism, but called themselves Sikhs. This way of life was, however, against the teachings of Guru Nanak. Guru Angad aimed to remove the confusion which Sri Chand had created among Sikhs.

GURU AMAR DAS (1552–74)

Guru Angad did not live long to guide his flock. He was just 48 years old when he died, after handing over the responsibilities of keeping the mission of Guru Nanak going to a man of 73 years of age, called Amar Das. Guru Amar Das was a distant relation of Guru Angad. He was attracted to Sikhism from Hinduism in his sixties through listening to the soul-stirring hymns of Guru Nanak recited by his nephew's wife, who was the daughter of Guru Angad.

Teachings

When he was a Hindu, Guru Amar Das often went on pilgrimages to holy rivers such as the Ganges to wash himself of religious and moral sins. The teachings of Guru Nanak, however, insisted on the cleaning of the inner self by prayers, meditation and good works. Guru Amar Das made his headquarters at Goindwal on the River Beas, not far from Khadur, and there dug a well with 84 steps leading down to the water level. He declared that whoever, after taking a bath in the *baoli* (well), would recite the *Japji* (the morning prayers of the Sikhs) once on each of the 84 steps would obtain release from the cycle of births and deaths. (See Chapter 6.) The idea gained popularity and helped in the spreading of Sikhism far and wide.

He appointed worthy Sikhs, including women, as missionaries to preach the new faith. He also introduced the custom of Sikhs gathering twice a year at Goindwal, on the days of Baisakhi and Diwali (see Chapter 7), so he could establish a close personal bond with every Sikh. It was made known that no one would be allowed to see the Guru and join in worship unless he or she partook of a meal in the *langar* first (see Chapter 11). Guru Amar Das is especially remembered for his pioneering work for the emancipation of women. He spoke against the custom of widows burning themselves to death on their husbands' funeral pyres, and encouraged widow remarriage among the Sikhs. He also laid down guidelines for Sikh funerals shortly before his death.

Guru Amar Das died at the ripe age of 95 years, naming his son-in-law, Ram Das, as the next Guru of the Sikhs.

GURU RAM DAS (1574–81)

After his marriage in 1553, Ram Das had actively supported his father-in-law, Guru Amar Das, for over 20 years in the organisation of missionary work. His own ministry, lasting for about seven years, is famous for two things. Firstly, he composed wedding hymns for the solemnisation of marriages and thereby relieved Sikhs from having to use Hindu scriptures and Brahmin priests for this. Secondly, he laid the foundations of the city of Amritsar in 1577 in the heartland of the *jat* peasantry of the Punjab. These people were favourably inclined to follow the simple Sikh teachings. They helped Guru Ram Das in the construction of water reservoirs with their free physical labour, and supplied grain for the *langar*.

GURU ARJAN (1581–1606)

Guru Arjan was the youngest son of Guru Ram Das. He was the first Guru to have been born a Sikh. He completed the excavation of the reservoir at Amritsar, and constructed a beautiful building called Harimandir (the house of God) in the midst of this artificial lake. He assembled a volume of the sacred writings of the Sikhs and installed it in the new building to serve as a focus of Sikh worship. A chain of small Sikh townships, such as Taran Taran, Kartarpur and Chherta Sahib, boosted further the image of Sikhism in the region. By the end of the sixteenth century the Sikhs had their own religious language, Gurmukhi, their scriptures and ceremonies, along with a central place of worship at Amritsar.

There was a sudden change in the religious climate of the country on the death in 1605 of Akbar, the Emperor of India. The Sikhs were accidentally embroiled in the political struggle between Akbar's son, Jehangir, and his grandson, Khusrau, for the capture of the Mughal throne.

The early Sikh townships in the Punjab.

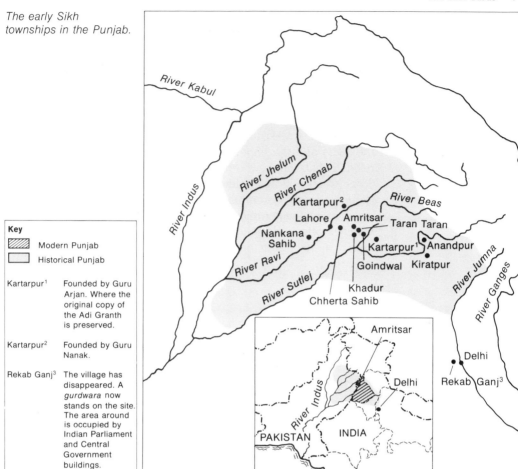

Key

▨ Modern Punjab

▢ Historical Punjab

Kartarpur[1] Founded by Guru Arjan. Where the original copy of the Adi Granth is preserved.

Kartarpur[2] Founded by Guru Nanak.

Rekab Ganj[3] The village has disappeared. A *gurdwara* now stands on the site. The area around is occupied by Indian Parliament and Central Government buildings.

Armed Struggle

Jehangir's inhuman and brutal treatment of the rebel soldiers and their commanders, torturing and partly blinding the rebel prince, Khusrau, and ordering the arrest of Guru Arjan and the seizure of his property, was in sharp contrast to Akbar's rule. Guru Arjan realised the danger to his life and so, before leaving Amritsar for Lahore to see the Emperor, he nominated his young son, Hargobind, to lead the Sikh community.

Guru Arjan fell a victim to the anger of the king, Jehangir, and tragically died in 1606 in Mughal custody. After that, the Sikh religion took a martial turn to fight for its survival.

?

1 Guru Arjan was the first Guru to have been born a Sikh. What advantages and disadvantages might this have had for him?

2 Imagine you are a Sikh who has just received news of Guru Arjan's death. Explain to a friend how your hopes for the future of Sikhism have given way to anxieties.

GURU HARGOBIND (1606–44)

Guru Hargobind took stock of the situation and resolved to prepare his followers to defend themselves adequately with force, if necessary. Guru Hargobind himself adopted the life-style of a soldier and maintained a standing army. He encouraged his Sikhs to ride and hunt. He was pleased to receive offerings of weapons and horses instead of money.

The Emperor ordered his detention for some years in the Gwalior fort for these warlike activities. There were a few skirmishes between the Sikhs and the imperial troops stationed in the Punjab in the reign of Shah Jehan, who ruled after Jehangir, but on the whole the Sikhs were not much interfered with by the authorities. Guru Hargobind also moved his headquarters from Amritsar to Kiratpur, which is in the foothills of the Himalayas and was outside the administrative jurisdiction of the Mughal officials. He passed away quietly in 1644 after nominating his grandson, Har Rai, to be his successor.

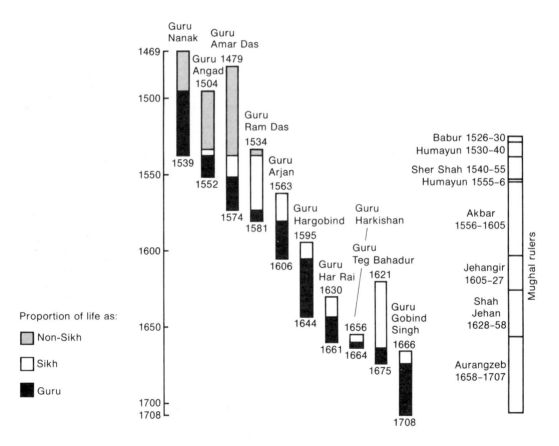

The Sikh Gurus in the Mughal context.

GURU HAR RAI (1644–61) AND GURU HARKISHAN (1661–4)

Guru Har Rai and Guru Harkishan devoted their energies to spreading the Sikh religion in the Hindu states of the north and strengthening it in the central Punjab.

The succession to the Mughal throne at Delhi had always had a bearing on official religious policy. When Aurangzeb (1658–1707) succeeded to the throne, he tried to impose the Muslim way of life on the Hindus and the Sikhs.

GURU TEG BAHADUR (1664–75)

Guru Teg Bahadur organised Hindu resistance to this policy of Islamisation (that is, the imposing of the Muslim way of life). Hindus and Sikhs protested because it impinged upon their religious liberty and freedom of worship. The Guru was arrested on charges of sedition and executed in Delhi in 1675. Few people stood by him but one Sikh, Jaita, of the sweeper (*chuhra*) caste, smuggled his head back to his family at Anandpur. Another, Lakhi Shah, a trader, rescued the body and took it to his village called Rekab Ganj. He could go no further as soldiers were in pursuit so he used his own home as a funeral pyre and cremated the body. A beautiful *gurdwara* (see Chapter 11) now stands on the site. The Guru gave up his life, but not his faith.

Anandpur, where the head of Guru Teg Bahadur was cremated.

श्री दसमेश पातशाह जी दे पवित्र समतर

What does this portrait tell you about the character and personality of Guru Gobind Singh?

GURU GOBIND SINGH (1675–1708)

The last of the ten Sikh Gurus also lost his life and family in the struggle he carried on against the repressive state policy, in defending the survival of the Sikh community. He did not nominate any human 'Guru' to succeed him but instead ordered his followers to look for spiritual guidance to the Guru Granth Sahib; that is, the scripture of the Sikhs (see Chapter 10). In all other matters they were asked to abide by the collective decision of the community taken in the presence of the Guru Granth Sahib and announced by their leader, called the *Jathedar*.

Guru Nanak's teaching formed the core of Sikh thought and conduct. Guru Gobind Singh created the Khalsa (see Chapter 3) to preach and practise them. Guru Nanak roused the people to regard social and political freedom as the birthright of every human being. Guru Gobind Singh showed them the way to achieve it.

The Gurus were eager to wean their disciples away from Hinduism. What steps did they take to do this? (List them Guru by Guru.) What reasons do you think they had for doing this?

Note The dates given for the Gurus in this chapter are the dates when they were Gurus and not the dates of their lives.

Chapter 3

The Khalsa

The Khalsa, a group or family of Sikhs devoted to the service of the Guru, was formed in 1699, but it is really the product of events going back almost a hundred years before that.

Sikhism is a practical way of life rather than a system of belief worked out in an armchair or a study. Its development has been shaped by history as well as by the genius of the Gurus.

When the Emperor Babur ill-treated prisoners and civilians during his conquest of the Punjab, Guru Nanak argued with him. Guru Amar Das persuaded Emperor Akbar to abolish taxes imposed upon Hindu pilgrimages to the town of Hardwar, and the same ruler reduced the land taxes on his subjects by one sixth when Guru Arjan appealed on behalf of the peasants.

Akbar's reign was one of great tolerance but this did not please all his Muslim subjects. Some felt that, as a Muslim, he should be using his power to further the cause of Islam. With his successor, Jehangir, their opportunity came. Within a year Guru Arjan had died a martyr's death. His son, the sixth Guru, Hargobind, kept a small standing army and was occasionally involved in an armed struggle against what were regarded as oppressive Mughal forces, especially in the days of the next Mughal, Shah Jehan. This ruler converted the *gurdwara* (see Chapter 11) in Lahore into a mosque and had some Hindus executed for marrying Muslim women.

With Emperor Aurangzeb the situation became even worse. In 1669 he issued orders to provincial governors for the destruction of the schools and temples of 'infidels'; that is, Hindus and Sikhs. Posts in the imperial service were closed to them and, in 1679, a poll tax which Akbar had abolished was reimposed. In 1675 Guru Teg Bahadur was executed in Delhi for organising resistance to this policy. Twenty years later an order was made forbidding any Hindus or Sikhs other than *rajputs*, a traditional warrior class, to ride horses or bear arms. Guru Gobind Singh (then known as Guru Gobind Rai) responded in 1699 by creating a Sikh brotherhood of arms as a challenge to the imperial policy.

THE NEW BROTHER-HOOD

On 30 March 1699 (which is 13 April by the modern Western calendar), the Guru summoned his Sikhs to meet him at Anandpur Sahib. The time was just before the spring harvest and the Punjab new year, Baisakhi. Addressing his followers, he asked one of them to come forward, ready to offer his life. For a time no one responded, being put off by the Guru's drawn sword and serious manner. Then, after repeated appeals, Daya Ram, a Kshatriya (member of the traditional ruling and warrior caste – see Chapter 17), came forward. He was led to the Guru's tent, there was a thud, and the Guru re-emerged, his sword dripping blood, and asked for another volunteer.

Perhaps surprisingly, five men in all did come from the crowd, but many others left or watched in silent fear. Besides Daya Ram, there was Dharam Das, a *jat* (that is, a member of a group whose traditional occupation is farming) who came from Delhi. There was Mukham Chand, a low-caste washerman, from Dwarka in Gujarat, and Sahib Chand, a baker from Bihar. Finally, there was a potter, Himmat Rai, whose home was at Jagganath in Orissa.

> **?**   Imagine you are Daya Ram. Tell a friend why you decided to go forward when Guru Gobind Rai asked for someone to be ready to offer his life.

After the Guru had taken the last man to his tent, he came out again, accompanied by the five of them, alive and unhurt. He told those Sikhs who remained that his action had been symbolic. In such times men must be willing to resist oppression even to the point of death. The five men were now dressed in clothes identical to his, saffron-coloured robes tied with a blue sash, and saffron turbans. 'My brothers,' he said, 'you are in my form and I am in yours. Whoever thinks there is any difference between us errs exceedingly!'

The Guru made a speech to the crowd. He said, 'In the time of Guru Nanak there was found just one devout Sikh. He succeeded Guru Nanak as Guru Angad. In my time there are five who are totally devoted to the Guru. These shall lay the foundation of Sikhism anew, and our religion will become famous throughout the world.' He said that these men would be the first five members of the new family of the Khalsa, and would be known as the *panj pyare* – the beloved five.

THE FIRST KHALSA INITIATIONS

Guru Gobind Rai told the Sikhs that he was introducing a new form of initiation ceremony. Until now, the ceremony had involved water being poured over a Guru's feet, caught in a bowl and drunk by the disciple. This ceremony was known as *charn-pahul*. From now on water would be put in a metal bowl, sugar crystals would be added to it and the mixture would be stirred with a double-edged sword, while certain hymns were recited. The ceremony would be performed by five Sikhs representing the *panj pyare*.

Those who were made members of the family of the Khalsa in this way had also to take certain vows. Khalsa literally means pure, and Sikhs who joined the family of the Khalsa were to try to do everything according to the teachings of the Guru. Besides keeping these rules Khalsa Sikhs were to have a common name, Kaur (princess) for women, and Singh (lion) for men. There were a number of reasons for this. The family name – for example, Sond, Johal, Patel, Sharma – indicates the caste group to which an Indian belongs (see Chapter 17). 'Kaur' and 'Singh' would remove this kind of distinction. They would also make people members of a new group in which caste was not to be important but which was recognisable by name. The names had a certain prestige and could be carried with pride. Women would have a standing of their own, known not as 'Mrs' or 'Miss' Singh, but as Kaur, a name derived from the group and not from a husband or father. The Guru himself became Gobind Singh and his wife Mata Sahib Kaur.

Amrit, the mixture of sugar and water blessed by the reciting of hymns, was prepared by the Guru assisted by his wife. He initiated the *panj pyare* who then admitted the Guru to the Khalsa by giving *amrit* to him.

Today not all Sikhs become members of the Khalsa. It requires a strict discipline that not everyone feels able to keep. Not all those who wear the turban and uncut hair have actually been initiated, but it is an ideal which most Sikhs intend to fulfil one day.

Guru Gobind Singh and his wife, Mata Sahib Kaur, preparing amrit *for the* panj pyare *at the first initiation ceremony, Baisakhi, 1699.*

1 How might it be claimed that Sikhs have cracked the feminist problem of women's surnames?
2 What reasons can you think of for Guru Gobind Singh deciding to form the Khalsa?

The Khalsa Vows

These are:
- to wear the five Ks (see below), and, in the case of men, the turban.
- to abstain from drugs and intoxicants.
- to respect women (no adultery or rape) – the violation of women is a common act of victorious armies.
- to follow the teachings of the Guru.
- to serve only the Guru, with arms if necessary and in a just cause.
- to reject caste differences and regard all Khalsa members as brothers and sisters.

INITIATION TODAY

Initiation is called *amritpan karna, amrit*-taking. It implies the taking of a number of vows at a special ceremony to regulate one's life in accordance with the rules and rites laid down in the Rahit Maryada (the Sikh Code of Conduct). Some historical *gurdwaras* (see Chapter 11) in India hold the ceremony at regular intervals several times a year; elsewhere it is held when called for.

The Ceremony of *Khande-da Amrit* (Initiation)

All the initiates, after taking a full bath, are equipped with the five symbols of the faith (see below). With five Khalsa Sikhs, called the *panj pyare*, they assemble together in the presence of the Guru Granth Sahib (see Chapter 10) at a place prepared for the performance of the ritual. Clean, fresh water, sugar crystals, a *khanda* (the double-edged sword), a *bata* (a steel bowl), a stand to hold it and the *karah prashad* (see Chapter 14) are the articles assembled before the ceremony begins. When everything is ready, a Sikh is put on guard duty so that nobody else may enter the room or the enclosure during the performance of the ceremony.

All the initiates are asked to stand up in front of the Guru Granth Sahib with folded hands. One of the *panj pyare* then explains to them the fundamentals of the Sikh faith. After obtaining their consent, this person will offer a prayer for the preparation of the *amrit* and a sixth Khalsa Sikh, acting as a *granthi* (see Chapter 10), will read the lesson from the Guru Granth Sahib.

Water and sugar crystals are poured into the *bata*, which is placed firmly on the stand. Each one of the *panj pyare* holds it with the left hand and stirs the mixture with the *khanda* in the right hand, while reciting the five prescribed scriptural compositions of the Gurus.

The panj pyare *preparing* amrit *for a modern initiation ceremony.*

The *panj pyare* sit in a special posture called the *bir asan*, with the right knee on the ground and the left raised. The five compositions of the Gurus are the *Japji* of Guru Nanak, the *Jap*, *Swayyas* and *Chaupai* of Guru Gobind Singh and the *Anand* of Guru Amar Das. These important hymns provide an admirable summary of the Sikh faith.

When *amrit* is ready, another prayer is offered. All the initiates are called to come forward one by one, made to sit in the *bir asan* posture, to receive the *amrit* in their cupped hands, to drink it and to say 'Waheguru ji ka Khalsa, waheguru ji ke fateh' (the Khalsa is of God, the victory is God's). This is repeated five times. Five times the *amrit* is sprinkled into their eyes and hair. When this is done they all stand in a line and are asked to sip the *amrit* from the *bata* in turn. This is followed by the recitation of the *Mul Mantra*, the first words of the Guru Granth Sahib, a number of times. Then one of the *panj pyare* will tell the new members of the family what to do and what not to do in their day-to-day lives. A final lesson is read by the *granthi* and all of those present are asked to share the *karah prashad* from one and the same bowl. This ends the ceremony.

What are the main elements in the initiation ceremony? What are the likely reasons for the ceremony being held in private?

The Meaning of Initiation

A child born into a Sikh family and brought up in accordance with the tenets of the Sikh faith is a Sikh. The initiation signifies a personal commitment to carry out all those religious and social obligations in words and deeds. Any sincere convert, regardless of background, race or colour, is accepted by Sikhism, but it has ceased to be overtly a missionary religion. The recent conversions brought about by Jogi Harbhajan Singh in North America, however, have come to all Sikhs as a pleasant surprise. The ceremony described above is the one which is used for converts as well.

The new members of the Sikh community are always given new names to bring them closer to the Punjabi Sikh tradition. For instance, John Dean could be called Daljit Singh after conversion.

SIKH SYMBOLS

There are five symbols, known in Punjabi as the *panj kakke* – the 'five Ks' – which every Khalsa Sikh must wear. Men must also wear turbans. Women need not but some do. The five Ks were made obligatory by Guru Gobind Singh but some may already have been worn by some Sikhs or the Gurus before 1699.

The Five Ks

1 Keshas – *uncut hair*

This symbol is a mark of dedication, holiness and group consciousness. The Sikh Gurus did not cut their hair and grew beards, as was often the custom among holy men. Many of their disciples would have followed their example.

In his Rahit Nama (Code of Conduct), Bhai Desa Singh, a follower of the tenth Guru, gave this reason for the uncut hair:

> God created the whole universe and then fashioned the human body. Man was given the beard, moustaches, and hair on the head. He who submits to God's will is firm in keeping them. Those who shave the head discard his will too. How will they find God in this world?

Bhai Nand Lal, another of Guru Gobind Singh's contemporaries, stressed the importance of the *keshas* in his Rahit Nama:

> Five Ks are the symbols of Sikhism, no exemption from them is possible. *Kara, kirpan, kacchas,* and *kangha*, without *keshas* are nothing.

Members of the Khalsa wearing the five Ks.

Even to trim the hair is an act of apostasy (departing from the faith). The Sikh congregational prayer, *Ardas*, contains the petition that 'each Sikh may be given the strength to remain steadfast in his faith to the moment of his last breath, and wear his sacred hair and symbols unmolested'. Anyone may worship in a *gurdwara* (see Chapter 11) but often the rule is that only those who keep the *keshas* may perform *kirtan* (that is, lead the singing) or sit in attendance on the Guru Granth Sahib.

2   Kangha – *the comb*
This is essential to keep the hair tidy. Cleanliness is an important principle of Sikhism. Daily bathing, regular washing of the hair and combing the hair twice a day are ways of ensuring this.

3   Kirpan – *the sword*
This weapon symbolises dignity and self-respect as well as a readiness to fight in the defence of truth or oppression. The initiated Sikh must always carry a sword in his or her belt. The sword may be up to three feet long or only a few inches, but it is always a weapon and never a charm to be worn round the neck or embedded in the comb, though this is how some Sikhs wear it.

The word *'kirpan'* should never be translated as 'dagger', for it is not a weapon that should be concealed or used with the stealth of an assassin or terrorist. If force is necessary it should be used openly, and only in a just cause. 'When all other means have failed it is right to draw the sword', taught Guru Gobind Singh.

4   Kara – *the steel bracelet*
This was not intended to be an ornament as it may appear today. Worn on the right wrist and probably thicker than those used now, it protected the sword-arm. Some Sikhs are reminded of the unity of the Khalsa or the oneness of God by it.

5   Kaccha – *short trousers*
In battle these were more practical than the *dhoti, lungi* or even baggy trousers often worn in the Punjab region. They are also more modest.

1   Objects can have both an everyday or practical purpose and a symbolic meaning. Some examples are a Manchester United scarf and a wedding ring! Explain their dual function and think of a few more examples.
   a What practical purpose did each of the five Ks once serve?
   b What symbolic purpose does each have today?

2   What are the advantages of an organisation having a uniform? Discuss with reference to a football team, a school, the navy, and an order of monks or nuns. What reasons might a Sikh give for wearing the five Ks and turban in the late twentieth century?

<table>
<tr><td>

Chapter
4

</td><td>

Rites of Passage

</td></tr>
</table>

Faithfulness and fruitfulness are the characteristics of a perfect marriage. The birth of a child strengthens the stability of marriage. It ensures the continuity of the family line and is thus a cause for rejoicing and thanksgiving. A couple of weeks after the birth, when the mother has fully recovered, the parents will visit the *gurdwara* to present the child before the Guru Granth Sahib (see Chapter 10). They will take with them a *romala* (a piece of brocade about a metre square) for the Guru Granth Sahib, and money to pay for making the *karah prashad*. These are the traditional gifts of thanksgiving. The *granthi* will offer *Ardas* (the general prayer) and invoke the blessings of God for the well-being of the child. He will also impress upon the parents the need to train and educate the child in such a manner that he or she turns out to be a good Sikh.

Choosing a Name

After the prayer, the Guru Granth Sahib is opened at random. The top hymn of the left-hand page is read out to the parents. The first letter of the first word of the hymn forms the initial letter of the name to be proposed for the child. Suppose the letter is 'J', the name then could be, for example, Jaswant, Jagdish, Jagmohan. The family decides the name and the *granthi* announces it to the congregation, adding 'Singh' for a boy and 'Kaur' for a girl, for their information and approval.

The *Anand Sahib* is then sung. A prayer of thanksgiving for the name is offered, *karah prashad* is distributed and the religious ceremony is complete. The name-giving can also form part of the regular weekly service of the *gurdwara*.

Amrit

Sometimes a *granthi* is requested by the family to give *amrit* to the baby. He will mix some sugar in water and will recite the first five stanzas of the *Japji Sahib* over it, while stirring the mixture with his short sword. When it is ready, he will dip the tip of the sword in the *amrit* and put some drops with it into the mouth of the child. The mother will be asked to drink the *amrit* which is left over.

A naming ceremony – the baby is given amrit *on the end of a* khanda *(double-edged sword).*

1 What is the significance of using the Guru Granth Sahib when choosing a name?

2 The birth of a baby is a time of hope and anxiety. Why? What kinds of anxieties might Sikh parents have about bringing up children in Britain?

3 Imagine you are a Sikh parent. Why would you wish to have a naming ceremony for a child rather than just giving it a name?

MARRIAGE

Marriage is a very highly commended institution in Sikh society. It is called *anand karaj* – the ceremony of bliss. It is entered into because the Gurus taught the importance of the family. Parents do not unnecessarily delay the marriage of their teenaged children after they have completed their education and are ready for marriage. With close relatives they not only cooperate in arranging and assisting the children in the selection of their marriage partners (see Chapter 5), but also contribute liberally towards the marriage expenses of the bride and the bridegroom. After marriage the couple continue to live at the home of the groom's parents as long as they wish, or as long as they are unable to set up a house of their own. A young bride, therefore, is expected to mould her habits and attitudes to fit into the new household and to endear herself to the other members of the family.

Betrothal

It is usual among Sikhs to have a formal betrothal ceremony. The bride's father, accompanied by a few close relatives, will meet the groom's parents and relatives to exchange presents for the bride and the bridegroom in the presence of the Guru Granth Sahib. This is meant to make the alliance public and to ensure that the promises made by the parties concerned are kept.

Fixing the Date

The date for the solemnisation of marriage is fixed according to the convenience of both parties. In India, however, weather is one of the factors that cannot be ignored, since the celebration takes place in the open air. This may be on the flat roof-top of the house, or in its courtyard, or in a park (*gurdwaras* – see Chapter 11 – are seldom used). Marriage celebrations are therefore avoided during the hot summer and the rainy season in the middle of the year.

The practice of determining the auspiciousness of the day chosen for the wedding by astronomical and astrological calculations is considered superstitious by the Sikhs. It is held that prayer offered to the almighty sanctifies all acts and all times. In Western countries most marriages take place on the weekends and usually in the *gurdwara*.

1 What factors determining the date of weddings should Sikhs ignore?
2 What factors might influence the date of a wedding in the Punjab but not in Britain?

Preparations

No document stipulating the respective duties and obligations of husband and wife to each other, or the committal of a specified sum of money or a gift of property to the wife in case of a divorce, is drawn up as a preliminary to the marriage contract. No oral understanding about the payment of a dowry to the bridegroom's father by the bride's parents or guardians is reached before the finalisation of the marriage arrangements. Such practices, prevalent among the major religious communities that surround Sikh settlements, are condemned by Sikhs.

The parents, of both the bridegroom and the bride, prepare numerous beautiful, costly dresses and order gold ornaments and jewellery for the bride, but within their means. The bride's parents and their relations load her with all sorts of useful presents and household goods, such as bedding, furniture and utensils sufficient to enable the couple to set up an independent home of their own.

The Reception

On the morning of the date agreed upon, the bridegroom and his party will reach the place decided by the bride's parents for the solemnisation of marriage. In India, it is generally the bride's parental home, but in the West marriages must take place in the *gurdwara*. Before sitting for the breakfast, a formal meeting between the fathers, grandfathers, and maternal uncles of the bridegroom and the bride takes place in the presence of the assembled guests. This is called *Milni*. The bride's side honour their counterparts with the presentation of turban lengths and a token gift of money. This is to reinforce the idea that a marriage unites two families and not just two individuals.

After the reception the guests gather together at the place where the Guru Granth Sahib is installed and form the congregation for the religious service to begin.

A bride and groom sitting in front of the Guru Granth Sahib.

The Religious Ceremony

Sikh musicians will sing hymns appropriate to the occasion and the bridegroom is asked to come forward and sit facing the Guru Granth Sahib. The bride follows soon after, decorated with ornaments and in a red dress, and is made to sit on his left-hand side. The *granthi*, or any other person known for his religious life, who is officiating at the function, will explain to the couple the responsibilities of a married life, and the respect they are expected to show to each other and to the other members of both the families. They are supposed to love and cherish one another, but are also reminded not to disregard the conventional, everyday expressions of courtesy for one another. Complete faith in the teachings of the Gurus, fidelity and faithfulness in conjugal life, righteous living and toleration and forgiveness for each other's faults are some of the other things which they are asked never to forget to practise. The couple will indicate the acceptance of the advice tended to them by bowing to the Guru Granth Sahib.

Thereafter the *granthi* will ask the couple and the fathers of the bride and the groom to stand up for prayers and to signify their approval of the proposed marriage. A lesson is read from the Guru Granth Sahib (also known as the Adi Granth – see Chapter 10) and the musicians sing this hymn:

> Before undertaking anything, seek the grace of God. By the grace of the Guru, who in the company of holy congregation expounds the truth, success is attained.
>
> Adi Granth 91

After these words, the father of the bride or the guardian who is to give the bride away will take the edge of the bridegroom's scarf and tie it to the edge of the bride's *dupatta* (long headscarf) and the musicians will recite the following hymn on behalf of the bride:

> Praise and dispraise, Nanakji, I let pass.
> I seize the edge of your garment, all else I let pass.
> All relationships I found false.
> I cling to you my Lord.
>
> Adi Granth 963

This is followed by the *granthi's* recitation of the first verse of the composition called *Lavan* or Marriage Hymn. When the reading of the passage is finished, the musicians sing it and the couple walk slowly round the Guru Granth Sahib in a clockwise direction with the groom leading the bride. They complete their circling of the Guru Granth Sahib by the time the musicians finish the singing. The couple bow to the Guru Granth Sahib before sitting down to listen to the second hymn.

A bride and groom circling the Guru Granth Sahib clockwise.

There are four verses in all, and the process is therefore repeated four times. The passages which are read and sung are the work of Guru Ram Das, and symbolise the spiritual union of the believer with God. Sikhs make use of them in the marriage service as an ideal to be kept in view in their married life.

The service is concluded with the singing of the *Anand* or the Song of Bliss – a composition by Guru Amar Das – by the whole congregation. After this, everybody stands up for a general prayer called *Ardas*. Then a final lesson is read and the *karah prashad* is distributed to all present. With it the religious part of the function is brought to a close and the social festivities begin.

Sikh social practices do not require the authentication of a wedding by a written statement approved by the community or the state. In Britain, however, Sikhs, like everyone else, comply with the law which requires the registration of a marriage. Most *gurdwaras* are licensed by the state to perform weddings. There civil and religious formalities are completed together by the officials appointed by the state.

1   How does the marriage ceremony remind Sikhs that the most important person present is God?
2   How does the ceremony show that two families, not just two people, are being united?
3   List the most important features of the Sikh wedding ceremony.

Separation and Divorce

A Sikh marriage can be defined as a religious sacrament because the Guru Granth Sahib is a witness to the marriage, and the promises and pledges taken by the couple in its presence about faithfulness to each other are regarded as binding on them. In actual practice, separation and divorce have been allowed to women by the community in case of desertion, habitual cruelty, insanity or impotence of the husband. The practice of divorce has now been legalised in India and elsewhere.

Polygamy

Polygamy has not been forbidden by the Sikh religious texts, and instances in fairly large numbers can be quoted to show its popularity with the aristocracy and the well-to-do. Even two of the Sikh Gurus, Guru Hargobind and Guru Gobind Singh, had more than one wife, and so had the Sikh rajas and maharajas. In the case of ordinary people, however, a second marriage was contracted only when the wife proved barren or failed to produce a male child, or when a man married his deceased brother's wife to give her protection and status. Since 1956 the practice of polygamy has been declared illegal in India and elsewhere.

DEATH

Whoever is born will cease to be.
If not today then tomorrow it may be.
Man may feel disturbed if anything unusual happens to him.
But in this world, Nanak, nothing is everlasting.

Adi Granth 1,429

When a person is about to die, relations and friends should try to divert his or her attention from worldly affairs towards God, and any demonstration of sorrow should not be allowed to intrude upon a peaceful going. The dying person should be encouraged to utter *'Waheguru, waheguru'* (wonderful Lord). It gives consolation to the departing soul at that psychologically important moment of life. As soon as the death occurs, one of those present should reverently close the eyes and mouth. The arms and hands should be extended on each side of the body. The body should be covered with a plain white sheet.

Sikhs recognise the place for natural feelings of sorrow and anguish and for their expression, but try to dissuade those who are hurt directly from weeping and wailing by consoling them and by quoting scriptures to them. For example, they remind them that 'It is God's will', and that 'Man comes by his will and dies by his will'. One of those present should recite *Sukhmani*, the Psalm of Peace, to discourage the family from indulging in extravagant displays of emotion. The relations and friends who are away are informed immediately and they try to reach the home of the bereaved as soon as possible. On the day of death, cooking is not done in the house; relatives bring in food and look after the children.

The Sikh dead are usually cremated, and the cremation takes place as soon as possible. Sometimes it has to be deferred to allow time for a post mortem or to await the arrival of a very close relative from abroad. In countries where facilities for cremation are not available, the Sikhs may bury their dead. It is also permissible to put the dead body into the sea or a river, and this is sometimes done in India.

The Funeral

Before the funeral the body is washed and clothed (complete with all the five symbols of the faith) by people of the same sex. The bier or the coffin is covered with the shroud – a plain cloth or a shawl.

The procession starts with a prayer and the mourners carry the bier slowly on their shoulders while reciting *'Waheguru'*.) Sometimes they carry it to the *gurdwara*, but more often directly to the crematorium. The services of the undertakers are utilised wherever they are available. A prayer for the peace of the soul of the dead person is said and the pyre is lit by a close relative. The *granthi* of the local *gurdwara* or one of the mourners will recite *Sohilla* (the bedtime prayer) and the *Ardas* (the communal prayer) while the corpse is consumed by the fire.

It is usual for the people who have been handling the body to take a bath before doing anything else, while others just wash their faces and hands. On returning home, a reading of the scriptures is commenced. A few pages are read and then the mourners leave the family, after taking *karah prashad*, and the normal activities of life are resumed.

Sometimes the arrangements for the reading of the scriptures are made at the *gurdwara*. The ashes are immersed in the running water of a nearby river.

Condolences

Friends and relatives continue to call in for a few days after the funeral to console the bereaved. The visits are short and the visitors sit on mats or carpets spread on the floor. The reading of the scriptures which is meant to provide spiritual support to the family of the deceased is completed in about ten days. Near and dear ones get together again for the final prayers in the afternoon on the day of the completion of the reading, and the condolence is closed.

After this, no ceremony or prayers whatsoever are ordained in Sikh religion. The erection of monuments in the name of the dead is strictly forbidden, to make sure that people do not worship them.

1 Describe a Sikh funeral.
2 The family plays a very active part in preparing and conducting a Sikh funeral.
   a What do its members do?
   b How do you think each of these things helps them cope with their grief?
3 Imagine you are a Sikh whose aunt has just died. Write a comforting letter to your uncle and cousins.
4 How might Sikh funeral rituals comfort mourners?

Chapter 5

The Family

The Sikh pattern of life defies rigid classification as a joint family system, an extended family system or a nuclear family system. It is certainly patriarchal, very hierarchical, and quite close-knit even when some of its members move out of the family in search of work and live away independently.

The Sikh pattern is in part a joint family system, because the family has often an ancestral common base to which its members return. It is in part an extended family system, because the members visit one another frequently, share the joys and sorrows of everyday existence among them and look after the elder members of their family. It is also a nuclear family system because, especially outside India, each family of parents and children has an independent home and keeps its own purse. The Sikh family is hierarchical because the senior members are consulted and their views are respected; when the discussion is over the decision is left to them. It is close-knit because the individual members help one another morally and financially in case of need.

The Community

Such a cooperative and corporate thinking finds expression in community living as well. The members of the kinship group and caste (see Chapter 17) form the congregation at marriages; support other members in any kind of legal troubles and stand surety for them; defend them even with their lives in case of a fight; provide them with a dignified funeral at death; and assist a surviving spouse and children until the children come of age.

1   What is a nuclear family?
2   What are extended and joint family systems?
3   How does the extended family operate as a support group for relatives in need?

Attitudes to Boys and Girls

'Is it a boy or a girl?' is the question asked by everyone on hearing about the birth of a child in a family. They are happy when it is a boy but not so pleased when it is a girl. Within a few days after the birth of a son, sweets are distributed among the relations and friends; but in the case of a girl, even simple good wishes are not always offered to the parents.

There are many causes of this attitude, some of them traditional. For example, the son is held to be more important than the daughter for the continuation of the family line, and is regarded as a potential wage earner. In a country without a social security system, like India, a boy is the support of his parents in sickness and old age. In a society in which women are traditionally not permitted to work outside the home, a girl is an economic liability; expensive to be brought up and married – after which she goes to live with her husband.

Boys enjoy considerable freedom to play and run about in the streets and fields, but the movements of girls are always restricted. In India, they spend most of their time within the house and the courtyard and are allowed to play outside only with children of approved neighbours and then within earshot of their parents. From early childhood they are taught to speak softly and politely to everybody and not to run about, shout or laugh loudly in the presence of elders.

1 List as many reasons as you can why Sikh parents have often preferred a son to a daughter.
2 What kinds of change in Indian society and parental attitudes will have to take place before girls can enjoy equality with boys?

Religious Upbringing

It is the responsibility of the parents to train children from an early age in the qualities and virtues that go into the making of religious

Why is the turban-tying ceremony often an opportunity for a family get-together and a party?

discipline. Children learn by imitation. If the daily conduct of the parents at home and in society does not match the ideals held before the children, how can the children be expected to imbibe godly qualities and righteousness?

Sikhs should not cut the hair of their children. They should be taught Gurmukhi at home or in the *gurdwara*, if it is not being taught at school. Wearing a *kara* (see Chapter 3) is not a problem. Children should also be persuaded to wear *kaccha* from an early age and the boys should be encouraged to wear a turban as soon as they can tie one. Children should be taken to the *gurdwaras* as often as possible. Active participation in the community activities could inspire them to go in for the Sikh initiation of *amrit*-taking (see Chapter 3).

Many young Sikhs hesitate to take *amrit* simply because they have not been saying their daily prayers regularly and not been wearing *kaccha* and *kirpan*. Social drinking is another habit which is not easy to get rid of in today's society. To enter into a highly moral and spiritual life of commitment, people need courage and conviction. That is why there are relatively few devoted and committed Sikhs initiated into the Khalsa, the pure ones.

?

Imagine you are a Sikh parent. How might living in Britain affect your attitude to bringing up your children? Why?

Education

Education in India is neither free nor compulsory, but the Sikh community there is quite well-to-do and can afford good education for its children. There are separate educational institutions for boys and girls. The few co-educational institutions are there to cater for special needs at a higher level.

In the UK, Sikh children go to state-run schools and colleges. Sikhs educated in the UK, whose parents in India may have worked on their farms or been in skilled jobs in industry, often become professionals (for example, lawyers or doctors).

ADOLESCENTS

After school, adolescent girls help their mothers in the kitchen and with other household chores. In their spare time they learn sewing, knitting and embroidery, and prepare dresses and other things which form part of their marriage trousseau. Some parents encourage them to go in for college education to keep their minds occupied. In the case of needy families, the girls take up suitable jobs to fill in the gap till their parents can find an appropriate match for them, and save money for meeting the marriage expenses.

Hair, Dress and Make-up

Among Indians, long hair is considered a sign of female beauty and much time is spent looking after it. Sikh women are under religious obligation as well not to tamper with their body hair. To give the hair extra length, cotton or silken braids called *dories* are used by young girls and housewives. Some married women, in imitation of Hindu women, wear a red spot in the middle of their foreheads and mark the hair-parting with red vermillion powders. All women, young and old, may wear gold jewellery, but unmarried girls are not allowed to wear rouge and lipstick – these are the symbols of a married woman. All women, young and old, are urged to dress modestly.

A Sikh should wear the uniform of the Khalsa, the five Ks and, in the case of men, the turban. Other than this any type of clothing may be worn, according to the climate and customs of the country. However, there is a concern that clothing should not be immodest or arouse sexual desire: 'Clothes should not be worn which cause pain to the body or breed evil thoughts', said Guru Nanak (Adi Granth 16).

SEXUAL MORALITY

Sexual matters are not discussed openly. Physical demonstration of love and affection in public, even between husband and wife, is not appreciated. Elder sisters and aunts, however, discuss the facts of married life freely with the teenage girls of the family who have reached puberty and are ready for marriage, but the virtues of remaining chaste before marriage are also impressed upon them.

Chastity is regarded very highly. Dating and courtship are out of the question. The pleasure of sex is to be confined to married life. The availability of contraceptives, therefore, is no reason for respectable Sikh youngsters to break with this tradition.

Contraception

There is no religious objection to married couples using contraceptives, but it is rare among newly-weds, for if the couple does not have a child within a year or two of the marriage their parents become anxious.

Abortion

Culturally Sikhs are akin to the Hindus, and they have always been considered to be a part of the wider Hindu community. The Hindu lawgivers treated induced abortion as a crime whatever the circumstances.

In 1969, the Indian Parliament reviewed the situation. Abortion has now been made legal on the grounds generally accepted as valid by many nations, including cases of rape and of pregnancy occurring as a result of failure of any device used by a married couple for the purpose of family planning. The highest religious authorities of the Sikhs, based in Amritsar in India, have never objected to the new legislation.

Why do you think Sikh parents hope that a young couple will have a child within a year or two of marrying?

MARRIAGE IN INDIA

India is a land of villages and a vast majority of its people make a living from the land, with agriculture as their main occupation. Industrialisation and urbanisation have just touched the fringes of this agrarian society, and the flow of life mostly continues undisturbed with its age-old ideals and institutions. People who migrate to the towns, or even go abroad, do not break the link between themselves and their relatives and roots.

The Conventions

In villages, most families are related to one another, and the young boys and girls are not allowed to mix, to avoid scandals. The boys and girls know that spouses for them are to come from other nearby villages and towns and that premarital romantic contact among them will only bring frustration and, if detected, might lead to feuds and revenge killings. Mere suspicion of a lapse can weaken the chances of a good marriage. Sensible boys well understand the consequences of breaching the social conventions and that they should therefore respect and treat the village girls as their sisters. Rural life with its very small degree of privacy needs such stringent attitudes to keep gossip at bay.

Restrictions

Relationship

There are restrictions prohibiting marriage with certain relatives and groups even if they are living away from the village. For instance, marriage between cousins is considered incestuous and marital union with the family of your father's sister, mother's sister and mother's brother is also regarded as undesirable. Marriage between two persons related within five generations on the father's side and three on the mother's is declared void.

Marriage alliances are established with families which are only remotely related and sometimes total strangers to one another, though they are often known to other family members and usually belong to the same caste. (See Chapter 17.)

Caste

The word 'caste' is synonymous with India. Caste is divisive. It perpetuates social inequalities of the worst kind, but it still persists. The extension of Hindu personal law to the Sikhs has dented the fabric of Sikhism as a casteless society. The effectiveness of recent legislation abolishing the caste restrictions in the selection of marriage partners is yet to be realised. Caste has further narrowed down the area of exploration for match-making. A young man dares not say 'I am going to marry this girl because we love each other' if the couple must then isolate themselves from their parents and the community at large because they are of different castes.

Region

Regional cultural differences play a part. People living in the southern districts of the Punjab, called Malwa, do not look for marriage partners in the northern regions, called Doaba and Majha.

Other Social Pressures

The life style and actions of a family in a small community, whether rich or poor, can be largely determined by the urge to win the approbation of neighbours and caste group within that community. 'What people will say' can become the motivation for all a family's efforts and aspirations, so that anything that would bring down the prestige of the family has to be hidden from the public view, and no effort is spared to broadcast any success that will enhance its esteem in the neighbourhood. The ostentatious display of a bride's dowry to impress wedding guests is, for instance, a common occurrence in north India.

Extravagant wedding celebrations are nothing but an excuse to display wealth and standing in public. People who want such displays are never satisfied with the bride's trousseau and some gold jewellery – the traditional parting gifts, or dowry, from the parents. They always look for more.

Dowries and dowry deaths

Dowry deaths are reported by the press as news, but they are not a new phenomenon. They have been going on for a long time. In India a newly married couple usually live with the husband's parents. Some in-laws will taunt the girl, saying that her parents have not given her enough cash and presents at the time of her marriage. The bride may be so continuously harassed that she is driven to suicide – a dowry death. Only recently has the government realised the enormity of such a crime.

The Prohibition of Dowry Act was passed by the Indian Parliament in 1961. This was followed by regulations passed by the Punjab government in October 1975 stipulating that no young woman who dies within seven years of marriage will be allowed to be cremated without a no-suspicion certificate from her parents.

The parents of the prospective brides, therefore, have to make sure, with the help of their friends and relatives, that their daughters will be treated well by their in-laws before concluding the marriage negotiations. The family's status in the social scale and its reputation are other factors that are taken into consideration.

1 What is a dowry?
2 Dowries are illegal in India but still persist. Can you suggest why dowries were made illegal? Why do you think they persist?

Arranging the Marriage

Within the framework of these essentials, once points of contact have been located and the details of a purely personal nature – such as age, appearance, accomplishments, and also moral character – are checked, face-to-face talks between the parents begin. An agreement is reached and the children are persuaded to accept it. Parents know their children well, and if they find that they have some reservations about the proposal, then arrangements are made to bring them together. The parents of the girl will invite the boy along with his family to their house for a cup of tea. The boy and the girl are given the opportunity to talk to each other and think over the proposal. After a few days, if there is any objection from either side or there is no proper response, the proposal is dropped and the search begins anew to find another party.

1 Why are most Sikh marriages arranged or assisted by the elders of the family?
2 What kinds of thing do you think Sikh parents would take into account when arranging a marriage:
   a for a son?
   b for a daughter?

MARRIAGE OUTSIDE INDIA

For Sikh communities that are settling abroad, especially in Western countries, the fulfilment of their cultural obligations is not easy. Their numbers are small and the places they have settled in are scattered, both facts which squeeze the choice of partners and the area of contact. Very often, therefore, they look for help to their relations and friends back home in the Punjab.

Social Pressures

Boys and girls who are allowed to come into a country as fiancé(e)s make news for the media. 'Here comes a boy or a girl from India who

Milni – *the fathers of the bride and groom meeting in front of the wedding guests.*

is going to marry so-and-so whom he or she has never seen even once before. How can it be possible?' the immigration staff ask; and their doubts about the stability of such a union are not ill-founded. They may be ignorant of the Indian way of life but they know their own culture well, and there is no denying the fact that many such marriages have not proved successful, owing to cultural and social differences not always being appreciated by the parents.

If the Sikh community outside India continues to insist on the observance of caste, clan and other matters which are part of the Indian scene alone, then it is sure to lose many of its young boys and girls through assimilation by marriage to other communities. These things certainly do not form part of the Sikh religion, but migrant communities are often very conservative culturally. Social distinctions based on the traditional hereditary occupations – *ramgarhias* (craftsmen) and *jats* (farmers) – have no real meaning in a society where the selection of work or occupation is determined by a wish to serve others, the opportunity of a good wage or a handsome profit, and not by birth. By obeying the Gurus' rule that a Sikh should marry a Sikh, without bothering about these other matters, we could make life much easier.

Many Sikhs still accept arranged or assisted marriages in Britain today, but some prefer the love marriages of their British friends. Imagine:
a you are a young Sikh who has accepted an arranged marriage positively. Explain your reasons to a group of friends who are not Sikhs.
b you are a young Sikh who wishes to reject arranged marriages. Discuss this with your parents and your sister, who had a successful arranged marriage three years ago.

Chapter 6

Life after Death

Almost all religions teach that death is not the end of human destiny, though their views about what happens after the end of earthly life vary from one another. The Sikh scriptures uphold the notion of the hereafter, as is evident from the following passages: 'One who indulges in sensuous pleasures here suffers miseries hereafter' (Adi Granth 1,276: Guru Nanak), and 'We get hereafter only what we give here out of our honest earnings' (Adi Granth 472: Guru Nanak).

Another assertion shared by many religions is that people are accountable to God for their actions. This is also supported in the Sikh scriptures, by such statements as: 'Our good and evil is scrutinised and judged in the presence of God, the Supreme Judge' (Adi Granth 8: Guru Nanak). In Sikh belief, however, the judgement takes place soon after the death of an individual and is not delayed till the end of the world. Sikhs are not certain that the world will eventually come to an end; only God knows. There is no fixed time for death: people may be called to account for their actions at any moment and the day of judgement is therefore every day.

HEAVEN AND HELL

The notion of heaven and hell also figures prominently in the content of the judgement – for instance: 'Heaven is not attained without good deeds' (Adi Granth 952) and 'Your name O God is the Formless One; by dwelling on it one does not go to hell' (Adi Granth 465). Scriptural passages such as 'In the deeps of hell is immense pain. The ungrateful wretches are cast there' (Adi Granth 315) and 'By mere talk of God you do not enter heaven. Deliverance comes only through truthful living' (Adi Granth 141/3) give the impression that heaven and hell are real places, located somewhere on this earth or hung in space, for meting out rewards and retributions. However, a careful further reading of the Sikh scriptures brings one to the conclusion that they are states of life and not geographical places in time and space: as Guru Arjan declared, 'My heaven is where the praises of God are sung' (Adi Granth 749/11), and 'In the midst of a myriad joys if one cherishes not the Lord's name, one lives as if in the deeps of hell. That place is no better than a waste land' (Adi Granth 707).

1   What should a Sikh do to 'go to heaven' when he or she dies?
2   Do Sikhs believe that heaven and hell are places or spiritual states?

REBIRTH AND TRANS-MIGRATION

After the judgement, the individual soul has to experience pleasure and pain, according to past actions, in the next form of life determined by God. Here the Sikhs share the Hindu belief in rebirth and transmigration of the soul (that is, the soul's being reborn in a different body): 'We inhabited several plants and trees and then reincarnated as animals. We were born as serpents of several species and then winged birds' (Adi Granth 156: Guru Nanak).

Rebirths

There are 8.4 million physical forms of lives, it is said. In one of his hymns, Guru Arjan described the various births of a soul:

The Jiva was born several times as a worm and a flying insect.
It was born several times as an elephant, a fish and a deer.
It was born several times as a bird and snake.
It was born several times as a horse and a yoked bull.
Meet the Lord, this is the opportune time.
After a very long time you have come in this body.
It was born several times as a stone and a mountain.
It was born several times as the lowest life forms.
It was born several times as plants.
It strayed into eighty-four lakhs of physical forms.

Adi Granth 176/10

How and in what sequence souls pass from one form of life to another has not been explained. What is clear, however, from many such utterances of the Gurus, is that the human birth is a rare opportunity and people should try to transcend the sufferings caused by repeated deaths and births, and this is only possible by turning to God. 'The vessel in which truth is not put is broken and remoulded' (Adi Granth 146), and 'Those who turn their backs on the Guru are born again and again as pigs and dogs. Fettered by their evil tendencies they come and go' (Adi Granth 832).

1 Do Sikhs believe that the soul only enters the body once or that it is reborn into a series of beings?
2 The reason for their belief is the teaching of the Gurus, but can you think of any arguments Sikhs might use to support their faith if they were discussing it with someone who did not share their views?

BELIEF AND ITS EFFECTS

The mind is drawn towards God either through the natural spiritual urge, or through the company of pious people, or through the Guru's word – that is, the scriptures. People imbued with the spirit of God are not afraid of death. They accept the will of God. A Sikh knows that 'From the beginning of time, pain and pleasure are written in man's fate by the creator' (Adi Granth 1,054/18), and so the ups and downs of life do not disturb the Sikh's peace of mind.

Sikhism teaches that one should not strive for salvation, paradise or a better life after death, but concentrate on doing good and resisting evil in all forms. 'If a man loves God, what does he care for salvation or paradise?' said Guru Nanak (Adi Granth 360/9). To see God is to see life as it really is.

?

How might faith in life beyond death help a Sikh cope with:
a day-to-day living?
b the death of a friend or relative?
c being told that he or she was suffering from an incurable illness?

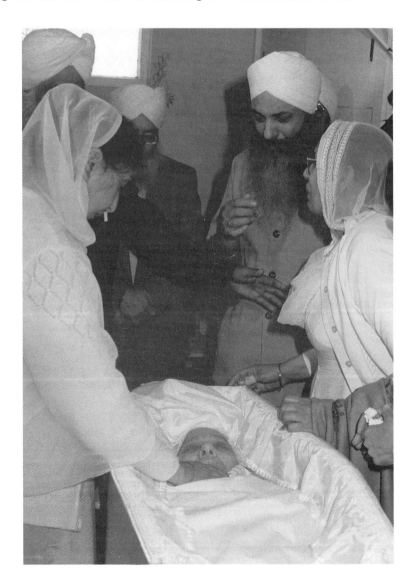

A family paying their last respects.

<table>
<tr>
<td>

Chapter

7

</td>
<td align="right">

Festivals

</td>
</tr>
</table>

Festivals provide a welcome break in the routine of life. The shared remembrance of a common past strengthens communal solidarity and cultural identity. Such occasions remind people of past achievements and encourage them to face the present and future with the same faith and spirit.

 Discuss what general reasons there are for having festivals, using such occasions as Spring Bank Holiday, Bonfire Night, and New Year as some examples to consider.

THE RELIGIOUS CALENDAR

The religious calendar of the Sikhs is not heavy. The only universal festivals are the birthdays of Guru Nanak and Guru Gobind Singh, the day of the martyrdom of the fifth Guru, Guru Arjan, and Baisakhi (see below). Diwali (see below) has become popular in Britain, but in India its observance tends to be confined to the Golden Temple at Amritsar. This type of limitation is true of other occasions as well. For example, the martyrdom of Guru Teg Bahadur is chiefly celebrated in Delhi, where he was executed, though Sikhs may come from beyond India to take part. There are many *gurdwaras* (see Chapter 11) dotted around the Punjab countryside which stand on a site made special by the presence of a Guru, like Batala where Guru Nanak was married. These may hold their own celebrations to commemorate such an event of local significance.

Sikh festivals are of two kinds: those which are connected with the lives of the Gurus, *gurpurbs*, and *jore melas*.

THE GURPURBS

Gurpurb means holy day in honour of the Guru. Its central feature is an *akhand path*, a continuous reading of the whole of the Guru Granth Sahib, which is usually arranged to last about 48 hours (spread over three days). A relay of men and women undertake the recital, no one doing a stint of more than two hours, for the reading must be clear and accurate. *Langar* (see Chapter 11) is served throughout this period and for the whole of the three days there will be a steady stream of villagers to the *gurdwara*. Those who do not do the reading will cook food, serve it, and keep the premises clean. Most of the community will be involved in one way or another.

The conclusion of an *akhand path* (it must end in the early morning) leads into a normal morning service, and any hymns composed by the Guru whose anniversary is being celebrated are an important part. There are also lectures and speeches explaining the importance of the event and the Guru's contributions to the Sikh faith. In cities this climax to the *gurpurb* may be held on a Sunday to enable the maximum numbers of people to participate and perhaps make it possible for notable speakers to be present.

The Procession

Sunday tends to be a weekly holiday, as Saturday afternoon often is. Schools close at 1.00 p.m. Saturday afternoon may therefore see the Guru Granth Sahib, carried on a lorry and preceeded by five men representing the *panj pyare*, parading through the town followed by brass bands, with children from Sikh schools and many members of the community singing some of the hymns from the Guru Granth Sahib. This is known as *nagar kirtan*. *Nagar* means a district or town, and *kirtan* is the practice of singing, hence the name. The procession will normally begin and end at a *gurdwara*.

THE *JORE MELAS*

Baisakhi, Diwali and Hola Mohalla are called *jore melas* – times for getting together. For most people they seem to be seasonal opportunities for enjoyment, often shared equally by Hindus and Sikhs. However, they do have particular meanings for members of the Sikh community. The first two were days when the Guru, from the time of Guru Amar Das, ordered his followers to join him wherever he happened to be. The purpose was to wean them from Hindu culture and help them reflect upon what it meant to be a Sikh. Guru Gobind Singh added a third, Hola Mohalla, as an alternative to the Hindu festival of Holi.

Preparing to raise the freshly covered nishan sahib *at Baisakhi.*

Singing kirtan (hymns) *at a London Baisakhi procession.*

Baisakhi – 13/14 April

On this day Sikhs are reminded that they are saint-soldiers who should be prepared to fight against injustice. In their assemblies the story of the first Baisakhi and the formation of the Khalsa is told (see page 12, The New Brotherhood). It is a popular time for young Sikhs to take *amrit* (that is, to be initiated), though the ceremony may take place at any time. Talks and lectures are given which encourage people to come forward for initiation, but also remind those who are already *amritdhari* (initiates) that they must keep the vows which they made perhaps many years ago.

The flag which flies over the *gurdwara*, the *nishan sahib* (see Chapter 11), may be renewed at Baisakhi. It is certainly likely that the cloth wrapped round the pole, the *chola sahib*, will be replaced. After being exposed to the weather for a year the old one will be dirty and probably torn.

The panj pyare *in a London Baisakhi procession.*

Other events which occurred on Baisakhi may also be called to mind. In 1801 at this time the Sikh leader Ranjit Singh assumed the formal title of maharaja. In 1919 the British General Dyer ordered his men to fire on a crowd in an enclosed space near the Golden Temple, called Jallianwala Bagh. There 379 men, women, and children were killed and over 2,000 wounded. For many Indians who had not yet made up their minds it was the act which made them join the 'quit India' campaign, aimed at making the British leave India.

Diwali – October/November

A number of events are connected with this day. In 1577, Guru Ram Das laid the foundation of the town which was to become known as Amritsar. His grandson, Guru Hargobind, was imprisoned by the Emperor Jehangir on treason charges, and released together with 52 rajas, whose freedom he had also secured, at Diwali. The beautiful illuminations at the Golden Temple in Amritsar are a reminder of those which greeted him on his return to his palace, the Akal Takht, which faces it across the artificial lake.

The eighteenth century was a period of almost endless persecution. In 1738 it seemed that there might be some respite for the Sikhs. One of them, Bhai Mani Singh, obtained permission for Sikhs to assemble at Amritsar, but on condition that a large amount of money was paid into the imperial treasury. The presence of a contingent of the Mughal army near the Temple deterred visitors so that the promised sum was not raised. Bhai Mani Singh was arrested and ordered to pay with his life unless he agreed to convert to Islam. On his refusal he was tortured to death. Seven years later bands of Sikhs gathered in Amritsar to form themselves into an army of liberation under the leadership of Nawab Kapur Singh. Their struggle resulted in the formation of the kingdom of Ranjit Singh some 60 years later.

These are the kinds of event which are remembered at Diwali. Those who cannot make the journey to Amritsar may place clay lamps on the doorsteps of *gurdwaras* or the garden walls or gateposts of their homes, and in the windows. Families often set off fireworks.

Hola Mohalla – March

At the Baisakhi assembly of 1699, Guru Gobind Singh established the Khalsa. The next spring he introduced a new custom, that of gathering in his presence at the time of the Hindu festival of Holi. Instead of joining in the celebrations associated with the Hindu god Krishna, Sikhs would bring their weapons and take part in military training manoeuvres. The name given to this third annual assembly was Hola Mohalla, which means 'attack and place of attack'.

A nihang at Hola Mohalla in Anandpur, northern India. Nihangs were traditionally warriors who guarded gurdwaras.

Today at Anandpur Sahib, where the first of these gatherings was held, after morning worship there are archery contests, mock battles, wrestling matches, and other martial activities. In Delhi and throughout the Punjab, funds are collected to help athletes to be trained and attend international competitions.

1   What general reasons for festivals apply to Sikh festivals?
2   Imagine you are one of the Gurus. What reasons might you have for wanting your followers to come to you at Diwali or Baisakhi?
3   Why do you think Guru Gobind Singh introduced the *jore mela* of Hola Mohalla?
4   What are the differences between a *jore mela* and a *gurpurb*? (Think of their meanings and their forms of celebration.)

Chapter 8

Pilgrimage

Pilgrimage to holy places is a characteristic feature of almost all religions, but it is not an obligatory duty for Sikhs, though they do go to visit the places connected with the origin and development of their history. God's name is the real place of pilgrimage and the knowledge of God through contemplation is learnt from the Guru. One who has absorbed the Guru's teaching, therefore, has no use for the places of pilgrimage.

EARLY GATHERINGS

In the early years of the Sikh movement, the followers went to see the Gurus for instruction and spiritual comfort wherever they happened to stay, in preference to the traditional Hindu pilgrim centres. The evidence for such early gatherings is available from the scripture: 'Wherever is my true Guru, blessed, blessed is that place. The devotees search out that sanctuary and apply the sacred dust of its precincts to their faces' (Adi Granth 450: Guru Ram Das).

The Sikh Gurus, however, were conscious of the importance which people attached to pilgrimage. Guru Nanak, during the course of his missionary tours, found it convenient to deliver his message to the people gathered at the places of pilgrimage. Guru Angad, before coming into the fold of Sikhism, was a frequent visitor to Jawala Mukhi, a place of pilgrimage in northern India. Guru Amar Das made several pilgrimages to the River Ganges, to bathe and be purified, before his conversion to Sikhism.

Preparing langar *at the Golden Temple, Amritsar.*

THE REASONS FOR PILGRIMAGE

The Sanskrit word for pilgrimage is '*tirath*', which means a ford or a bathing place, and most of the places of pilgrimage are therefore located on the banks of rivers and lakes. Many people believe that by just taking a bath at the sacred places they are sure to be absolved of all their sins and helped to cross from this world to the next.

Sikhism strongly denies any such suggestion that salvation can be attained by any sort of ritual purification of the body. The Sikh scriptures are clear: 'True pilgrimage consists in the contemplation of the name of God' (Adi Granth 687), and:

> If a man goes to bathe at a place of pilgrimage with the mind of a crook and the body of a thief his exterior will of course be washed by bathing but his interior will become sullied twice over. He will be cleaned from without like a gourd but he will be cherishing pure poison within. The saints are good even without such ablutions. The thief remains a thief even if he bathes thus at places of pilgrimage.
>
> Adi Granth 789

How is it, then, that Guru Amar Das constructed a *baoli* at Goindwal? This *baoli* was a deep well with 84 steps leading down to the water level, signifying 84 lakhs (hundred thousand rounds) of existence. Why did Guru Ram Das dig a bathing tank at Amritsar? Also Guru Arjan, while extolling everything associated with the life of Amritsar, said that 'Whoever bathes in your pool is rid of his sins' (Adi Granth 1,362).

The entrance to the baoli *at Goindwal.*

Adapting Traditional Ways

Are these to be regarded as departures from Guru Nanak's clear rejection of Hindu purificatory rites? Or are they to be seen as calculated steps to adapt a deep-rooted popular belief and give it a new direction?

With the completion of the *baoli* the word went round that whoever, after taking a bath in the *baoli*, recites the *Japji* (the Sikh morning prayer) 84 times, once at each step, will attain emancipation from the cycle of births and deaths. This was not a cheap way to salvation but only a recipe for recitation of God's name. It was meditation, not bathing, that mattered. Guru Arjan's advice, 'After taking a bath meditate on your Lord, and your body and mind become pure' (Adi Granth 611), is also clearly meant to shift the emphasis from the body-washing to the contemplation of God.

> The man who bathes in the ambrosial water of the divine knowledge takes with him the merit of bathing at the sixty-eight holy places of Hindu pilgrimage. In the Guru's teaching are the priceless jewels of virtue: whosoever follows the Guru's word can discover and possess them. There is no place of pilgrimage equal to the Guru's. The Guru alone is the pool of contentment. The Guru is the river whence pure water is ever obtained, by which the filth of evil understanding is washed off.
>
> Adi Granth 1,328: Guru Nanak

In a time when people were flocking into the fold of Sikhism, it was necessary to provide for traditional needs and then teach the people new ways.

1 Imagine that you are a young British Sikh who has never visited India. Your grandparents send you a return ticket to spend the Christmas holidays with them, and visit Amritsar and other places linked with the lives of the Gurus. What kinds of feelings would go through your mind as the day of departure drew near? Why would you want to go to the Punjab?
Write a letter to your school friends about your visit to the Golden Temple.
2 Some Sikhs do not approve of pilgrimages. Suggest reasons which they might put forward to support their view.
3 How did some of the Gurus try to provide for traditional needs so that they could then teach people new ways?

<table>
<tr><td>Chapter
9</td><td>*The Guru and the
Gurus' Teachings*</td></tr>
</table>

The idea of attaching oneself to a spiritual preceptor called the Guru is a recognised feature of Indian spiritual tradition. In the absence of an organised religious teaching such as that provided by churches and their ministers in the West, the people had to look for guidance wherever they could find it; and in their search for a Guru they sometimes stumbled into making a wrong choice, which led them to disillusionment in the end. So while emphasising the need for and importance of a Guru, the Sikh scriptures have provided the seekers of truth with adequate guidelines as well, to enable them to make a right selection: 'Go to the Guru who confirms you in truth, makes you talk of the indescribable and unites you with the word' (Adi Granth 686), said Guru Nanak. The disciples are further advised 'to act on the word of the Guru and not to ape his actions blindly' (Adi Granth 933: Guru Nanak), because, as Guru Amar Das said, 'it is through the Guru's word that one mounts to one's God. Without the word the world is led astray and is punished at God's court' (Adi Granth 600).

A Sikh artist's impression of Emperor Akbar taking langar *before meeting Guru Amar Das.*

THE ROLE OF THE GURU

The word Guru comes from 'Gu' meaning darkness, and 'ru' meaning light or revelation. The Guru, therefore, is a dispeller of darkness or ignorance and a revealer of light or right understanding – in short, an enlightener. Only a soul that has reached perfection can awaken the love of God in others:

> He whose heart is illumined and who has no attachment to the other is, O Nanak, the Guru. Meeting with him one is emancipated because the Guru makes him sing the praises of God.
>
> Adi Granth 168/22: Guru Ram Das

In theory all human beings are potentially capable of God-realisation (see Chapter 13) because 'God resides in the soul and the soul in turn is contained in God' (Adi Granth 1,153), but in actual practice, most people are not used to thinking for themselves. They therefore look for some tangible spiritual support. Reason alone does not always help to refine and purify one's thinking, whereas by following the example and guidance of a life that has experienced spiritual happiness one can rise above one's own desires and inclinations. 'You can light your own lamp from a lamp that is already lit,' it is said:

> There is light among all and that light is God's own self, which pervades and enlightens everyone, but it becomes manifest only through the teaching and the leading of the Guru.
>
> Adi Granth 663/18: Guru Nanak

People engrossed in the day-to-day affairs of life seldom find time to reflect on what is right and what is wrong for them. Filled with the love of family, greed and personal ambitions, one often forgets one's obligations and responsibilities towards one's fellow humans:

> Man is awake and yet he is being robbed. The worst of it is, that he is enjoying it. He is wearing the noose of worldly attachments round his neck and he is becoming more and more involved in them.
>
> Adi Granth 1,330

The spiritual knowledge and moral training essential for virtuous and noble living can only come from associating with godly people. Such people in Sikh terms are known as *Gurmukhs*, God-oriented.

1   What is a Guru?
2   Sikhs sometimes say that 'Gu' and 'ru' both have meanings of their own. What are they? How do they help people to understand the work of a Guru?

The Word of God

The transformation in the personality of the disciple is, however, effected with the help of the word of God, called *Bani* or *Shabad*. The word of God means the message, the revelation, which comes from

God. The Guru is just a channel of its mediation. 'The true Guru is the Word. The Word is the true Guru; that shows the path of liberation' (Adi Granth 1,310/3), declared Guru Ram Das. The Guru is therefore revered not for his person but for what he does.

Individual Effort

It should be remembered here that the Guru is only a guide. 'The Guru is the ladder, the boat, the raft by means of which one attains to God' (Adi Granth 17), but the initiative always rests with the individual. The Guru provides the means, the individual has to make the necessary effort.

No true Guru would encourage his disciples to worship him. God alone is to be worshipped. The fallacy of attaining the grace of God by merely serving the Guru has also been rejected by Guru Amar Das in strong words:

> The whole world enjoys the sight of the Guru
> But none will be saved by merely the sight of him.
> One must mould one's thoughts according to the Guru's words,
> Otherwise the charge of self-centredness will not be removed
> Nor will his love be fixed on God.
>
> Adi Granth 594

It is evident that every individual has to work out his or her own salvation. No one else can do it.

The Enlightened

Also the possibility of a disciple becoming as enlightened as the master cannot be ruled out. The following hymn of Guru Amar Das clearly shows that it can happen:

> Nanak, behold this pleasure:
> From the Guru came into being another Guru.
> The creator caused it to be so.
> The light has blended with light.
>
> Adi Granth 490/18

When the disciple has reached this stage of bliss, then no difference is left between the Guru and the disciple:

> The Guru is in the Sikh, the Sikh in the Guru,
> For both promote devotion to God.
>
> Adi Granth 444/8: Guru Ram Das

Such souls are called *Jivan Mukat*, liberated while alive. They are perfect examples of saintliness, and work for the good of others:

> Above birth and death are thy saints, for they come into the world to do good to others, and they bless all with the life of the soul and lead all to thy worship and unite all with thee.
>
> Adi Granth 749/2: Guru Arjan

Imagine you are a Sikh parent. What arguments would you put forward to encourage your daughter or son to attend Gurmukhi classes?

GOD AS SUPREME GURU

In the Sikh scripture, the word Guru has been used by Guru Nanak and his successors for God as well: 'Creating all, O God, thou art the supreme Guru. I am devoted to thee and bow before thy feet' (Adi Granth 1,187/15: Guru Nanak), and 'The transcendent Lord, God, is the Guru whom Nanak has met' (Adi Granth 599/6). Like Guru Nanak, other Sikh Gurus too had direct communion with God: 'My Guru is eternal. He is neither born nor dies' (Adi Granth 759/7: Guru Ram Das), and 'Listen, the eternal God, the Lord is my Guru' (*Benti Chaupai* [part of the evening prayer] 9/3–4: Guru Gobind Singh).

Enlightenment comes from God, who is therefore the Guru of all, including the ten Sikh Gurus. It is also clear that a human Guru is not essential for the mystic achievement. But there is no denying the fact that the help and guidance of a *Gurmukh* (God conscious person) makes it easier to reach the goal: 'In the company of a God-oriented person, everyone is liberated' (Adi Granth 273), and 'He is himself liberated and liberates others too' (Adi Granth 195).

It is this sort of thinking that encouraged the mushroom growth of Gurus and godmen of all sorts in India. In the Punjab, saints are a dime a dozen, it is said. The sheer wisdom and organisational skill of the Sikh Gurus, however, kept Sikhism from falling apart into rival groups.

1   Sikhs call God the Guru. What do they mean by this?
2   What are the most important differences between the ten human Gurus and God as Guru?

THE *GURBANI*

The word *Gurbani* means the Word, the sayings or the teachings of the Gurus that form the basis of Sikh religion. Saints and seers, when absorbed in the contemplation of the divine, try to seek an answer to the problems of life, conditioned as it is by an ever-changing ideal and environment. The guidance provided by them, which is based on their personal, spiritual experiences of a purely non-sensory nature, is termed 'revelation'. Guru Arjan's observation that 'Everyone has a vision of God according to the light granted to him' (Adi Granth 275) points out the limitations to which such an experience is exposed.

While acknowledging the relevance of the past revelations, the emergence of the new ones is clearly recognised in such Sikh statements as this: 'Namdev, the calico printer, and the Kabir, the weaver, attained the exalted state through the true Guru. Deeply spiritual men chant their words, none can efface them, brother' (Adi Granth 67/12). In Hindu society these were men of low caste (see Chapter 17) who could not even study the Vedas, the Hindu scriptures.

The Process of Revelation

Sikhs believe that revelation is a continuing process: 'Holy is the word. Holy the sacred texts. Through holy teachers it is uttered age after age' (Adi Granth 424: Guru Amar Das). The idea of a last messenger or the final word from God is therefore ruled out.

The Sikh Gurus were not just the passive channels of divine revelation, however, but also God-fearing men actively engaged in dealing with the physical and spiritual discomforts of the people around them. At crucial moments the Word of God descended upon them as suddenly as the rain from above. It is in this sense that their utterances were divinely inspired. On one occasion, Guru Nanak declared to a disciple of his called Lalo that:

> As the word of the Lord [*Gurbani*] comes to me
> So do I utter it, O Lalo.
>
> Adi Granth 722

Elsewhere Guru Arjan confesses: 'I do not know what to say. What I say is what my Lord commands' (Adi Granth 763). So saying that their utterances are the words of God does not seem to be inappropriate. In the voices of saintly men we hear the voice of God. It is in this sense that 'The Guru's word is God himself, through the word union is achieved' (Adi Granth 39: Guru Amar Das) and 'wonderful, wonderful are the words which denote the formless Lord' (Adi Granth 515: Guru Amar Das).

The message of the Gurus possesses an eternal value but the current situation gives special content to their utterances. 'When sages speak about a particular person, the moral is for the whole of humanity' (Adi Granth 647), said Guru Amar Das. Thus Sikhism recognises the fact that every prophet or revelation provides a path to God-orientation. The Sikh Gurus in their turn tried to clear the path of hurdles and pitfalls to make the journey a little more comfortable.

1   What do Sikhs have in mind when they use the word 'Gurbani'?
2   Why do Sikhs believe that God speaks to humanity through other people, not just through the Sikh Gurus?

<table>
<tr><td>

Chapter

10

</td><td>

The Scripture

</td></tr>
</table>

GURU GRANTH SAHIB

The Guru Granth Sahib is the main scripture of the Sikhs. Its first title, the Adi Granth (which means primary and original), clearly signifies its importance in Sikh faith and worship.

The Form of the Guru Granth Sahib

The Guru Granth Sahib (or Adi Granth) is an enormous volume of 1,430 large-size printed pages in a script called Gurmukhi. Each printed copy is identical. If you turn to page 10 or 1,000 of any copy you will find the same words written, even when the type and size of the page vary from the standard edition used in the *gurdwaras* (see Chapter 11). In this book, for example, 'Adi Granth 91' after an extract means that the quotation is from page 91 of the Adi Granth, and 'Adi Granth 141/3' means that the quotation is from line 3 of page 141. 'Adi Granth 1,276: Guru Nanak' means the quotation is from page 1,276 and is by the founder of the Sikh religion, Guru Nanak, himself.

Reading from the Guru Granth Sahib in a gurdwara in Coventry.

The style of language used is poetry, but there are many forms of versification. The hymns are not arranged by subject or author, but divided into 31 *ragas* (musical measures) in which they are meant to be sung. At the beginning and at the end, however, there are small sections of devotional readings from morning and evening services. These provide an epilogue to a complete reading of the scripture, and are meant for recitation only.

Under each *raga* the hymns of the Gurus in order of their succession come first, and then of the other holy men beginning with two Muslims, Kabir and Farid. The number of contributors varies from section to section. There are at least 15 poets whose total contribution comes to only 36 hymns. Five of these poets have only one hymn each to their credit. Guru Arjan's contribution is the largest at 2,218 hymns, followed by Guru Nanak (974) and Guru Amar Das (907). Among the saint-poets Kabir comes first with 541 hymns. There are nearly 5,900 hymns in all in the Adi Granth. Some are very short, others are several pages long.

The History of its Formation

This is to be traced back to the revelations of Guru Nanak and the hymns of the other saintly persons collected by him during the course of his missionary journeys in India and abroad – men like Kabir and Sheikh Farid, who have already been mentioned. Guru Angad, his immediate successor, helped Guru Nanak in copying out the hymns for the use of the scattered Sikh communities. He also committed his own utterances to writing, but there are only 62 of them. Guru Amar Das added his hymns and commissioned his grandson, Sahansar Ram, to put the sacred material into a number of volumes, later known as 'Mohan Pothis', because they were kept by Baba Mohan, the elder son of Guru Amar Das.

Guru Arjan was an excellent poet and he contributed the largest number of hymns to the Sikh scripture. But Sikhs regard the crowning glory of his achievement as being the compilation, in 1604, of the entire collection into a single volume. He had the works of his father, Guru Ram Das, in his possession and he had no difficulty in obtaining the Mohan Pothis. The original Adi Granth is carefully preserved and can be seen in the *gurdwara* Shish Mahal at Kartarpur in the Punjab, northern India.

A century later, in 1704, Guru Gobind Singh prepared a second version of the Sikh scriptures by adding the hymns of his father, Guru Teg Bahadur, and gave it the status of Guru before his death in 1708. It is this revised edition of the Adi Granth, the Guru Granth Sahib, which is the focus of attention of the congregation in the *gurdwaras* today.

The Harimandir (Golden Temple)

Soon after its compilation in 1604, the Adi Granth was installed in the Harimandir, at Amritsar. It is a specially designed building constructed in the midst of an artificial lake called a *sarovar*. This act

What thoughts might be going through the worshipper's mind as he bows in front of the Guru Granth Sahib?

of installation is regarded as a landmark in the development of Sikhism. The central collection, with its public readings, gave the Sikhs the day-to-day rules of religious and moral conduct, and a source to refer to against fake hymns issued in the name of the Sikh Gurus by rival groups. It also discouraged over-enthusiastic copiers and preachers from altering the authorised text. The Granth was installed on a raised platform called a *takht* (throne) under a canopy. Baba Buddha, a very old man who had become a follower of Guru Nanak as a boy, sat behind it with a *chauri* (a fan symbolising authority) to recite the scripture. The devotees formed the congregation. Guru Arjan, like everybody else, bowed before it in reverence and sat on the floor among them. This has been the form of Sikh worship ever since.

Granthi, perhaps holding *chauri*

Palki

Manji Sahib (stool) on which Guru Granth Sahib is placed

Guru Granth Sahib

Ragis

The throne of the Guru Granth Sahib.

Karah prashad in metal bowl

Money offerings

Offerings of milk, fruit etc.

Takht

Writings of Non-Sikhs in the Scripture

A characteristic feature of the Sikh scripture which sets it apart from every other holy book is the inclusion of selections from the writings of some prominent non-Sikh saints of widely divergent religious persuasions. Some belong to an earlier age and others were contemporaries of the Gurus. Muslims like Kabir, Farid and Bhikhan, and Shudras or low-caste Hindus like Ravidas and Nam Dev, find their place along with the high-caste Hindu Brahmins like Jaidev and Ramanand. (See Chapter 17 for an outline of the caste system.)

In everyday life these people, coming from communities of diverse faiths and imbued with the notion of high and low, do not mingle for worship or social purposes. Sikhs should have no such reservations. Anyone, irrespective of religious affiliations, can participate in the Sikh worship. Truth is not the monopoly of any one religion and the grace of God is available to anyone who loves God and his creatures: these are the ideas that seem to have weighed with Guru Arjan when he was sifting through the compositions for editing. Guru Arjan said

'The four castes of Kshatriyas, Brahmins, Shudras and Vaishyas are equal partners in divine instruction. Nanak, he who dwells on the name of God alone is emancipated in this age' (Adi Granth 747/18). The Guru Granth Sahib thus commands a unique position among the holy books of the world.

?

1   Write the following paragraph in your notebook, filling in the blanks. The Guru Granth Sahib is written in a script called _____. Printed versions are always _____ pages long, but old handwritten copies varied in size. It is divided into _____ sections known as _____. Each section begins with the hymns of Sikh _____. Most are by _____ _____. Two non-Sikhs whose compositions are included in the Guru Granth Sahib are _____ and _____. Altogether there are nearly _____ hymns in the book. Sometimes it is called by another name, the _____ _____.

2   Discuss why Guru Arjan decided to compile the Adi Granth. List what you think are the most important reasons.

3   Sikhs may have wondered which was the more important, Guru Arjan or the Adi Granth. How did he show them?

4   **a** What reasons might Guru Arjan have had for including the writings of non-Sikhs in the Adi Granth?

    b What does this tell us about the Sikh attitude to other religions?

THE PLACE OF THE GURU GRANTH SAHIB IN SIKH LIFE

The Guru Granth Sahib is the most highly prized possession of the Sikh faith. Great respect is shown while handling it. It must be opened in the morning with a prayer before the worship begins and closed at night, when nobody is expected to read it, with the recitation of evening prayers called *Kirtan Sohilla*. It is the focal point of worship in the *gurdwara*, and calls for special attention and time from the family if a copy of it is installed in a room at home or is borrowed from a *gurdwara* temporarily for a special reading.

The Guru Granth Sahib stands witness to the important stages of life of a Sikh. In its presence a Sikh child is named, initiated into the order of the Khalsa and married. At death the relations recite it to seek consolation and to pray for the peace of the departed soul. This may look to a sceptic just a social conformity; to a devotee, to read or listen to the Guru Granth Sahib is to talk to the Gurus themselves and to seek their blessings and encouragement to bear with the vicissitudes of life. 'True happiness lies in sharing your innermost thoughts with God', said Guru Amar Das (Adi Granth 850).

The congregation stands up when a copy is brought in at the start of the service or is taken away to its resting place. It is always carried on the head. When the Guru Granth Sahib becomes too worn to be read, it is cremated and the ashes are thrown in a river.

The Guru Granth Sahib may be kept in a special case like this one.

1   How do Sikhs show respect for their scriptures?
2   Make a list of the family and community activities which take place in the presence of the Guru Granth Sahib. You should be able to think of four or five – look back to earlier chapters.
3   Sikhs believe that the Guru Granth Sahib is the most highly prized possession of the Sikh faith. A Sikh friend spent two weeks' wages on buying a copy, decorating, carpeting, and fitting out a room to put it in.
    a   Imagine you are that Sikh. Write to a friend explaining why you did it.
    b   He had longed to do this for 20 years. Can you suggest reasons why he hadn't done it sooner? (Clues: respect, space, time, cost.)

THE GURU GRANTH SAHIB'S TEACHINGS

The primary concern of the Sikh Gurus was to offer people basic guidance on how to live a good and meaningful life. The approach is direct and practical. To meet human spiritual needs, worship of one God called the Akal Purkh is emphasised and idolatory in all forms is denounced. Meditation, prayers and worship are based on the teachings of the Gurus and no faith is to be placed in any other religious texts, so that the devotees do not stray from the path laid down for them by the Gurus. The attributes of God are to be remembered. Prayers must be offered and worship performed, both individually and collectively. Recitation or singing of the Gurus' hymns to the exclusion of all other ceremonies and rituals is the method recommended for it.

Basic Guidelines

Family life is considered superior to celibacy and asceticism. The world is full of all sorts of temptations; for an average person it is difficult to keep the character free from blemish. Married life is therefore recommended as the norm, so that family members may support one another. Every able-bodied person is encouraged to work for a living and then share the fruits of labour with the needy. Human equality has been recognised, and discrimination of all sorts, whether based on race, religion, sex or status, stands condemned. Women have been given an honoured place in both religious and social spheres.

Historical Aspects

The Adi Granth also provides insights into the religious, political and social conditions prevailing in India during the middle ages. The hymns in the Guru Granth Sahib represent nearly five centuries of Indian religious thought. There is no direct reference to historical events except one, that of Babur's invasion of India. There is a graphic description of the destruction wrought by the army and Guru Nanak's admonition to the selfish rulers of the country (Adi Granth 417).

Another notable exception is the account of the last moments on earth of Guru Amar Das by Bhai Sunder (Adi Granth 923–4). It serves as a precedent for the Sikhs as to how they should conduct the funeral rites of their dead. But no biographical information about the lives of the Gurus is given.

Language and Translations

During the Guru period (1469–1708) Muslims were the rulers of the country and Persian was the administrative language of the state. Arabic was used for religious purposes. Many Persian and Arabic words of everyday use crept into the writings of the Sikh Gurus, whose vocabulary was mainly drawn from Hindi language and literature. Saint-poets wrote in Sant Bhasha, which is akin to Hindi.

The passage of a few centuries has not rendered the Guru Granth Sahib obsolete or difficult to understand. Sikh children learn to read it in the schools and colleges which they attend. The phrases and sayings of the *Gurbani* (see Chapter 9) are used to embellish the Punjabi language and literature. Many of the teachings in its hymns have become popular proverbs, such as 'Falsehood exhausts itself. Truth alone prevails ultimately' (Adi Granth 953/21), and 'Unpretentious sweetness and humility is the essence of virtue' (Adi Granth 470/18).

Complete versions of the Guru Granth Sahib are available in Hindi, Urdu and English. In Canada a French-language version has just been produced. The Guru Granth Sahib is still read and taught everywhere by the Sikhs in the original Punjabi language and this has contributed to Punjabi remaining as a language of prayer and worship. For non-Punjabi-speaking people, translations are of enormous value, but they are not likely to oust the Punjabi, at least for some time to come, from its pride of place as the vehicle for the authentic sacred text.

Translations of the Guru Granth Sahib are available, but only copies in the original language are used in rituals. What reasons can you suggest for this?

DASAM GRANTH

Among the sacred scriptures of the Sikhs, the Dasam Granth comes next to the Guru Granth Sahib in importance. Guru Gobind Singh, the last of the Gurus, was a great writer and poet. He wrote in a number of languages, including Hindi, Persian and Punjabi. Like the other Gurus' his poetry was religious, intended for meditation and spiritual development. However, he was also modest to the point of not including any of his works in the Guru Granth Sahib when he added those of his father.

The material was assembled by a follower of the Guru, Bhai Mani Singh, and published in 1734, 26 years after Guru Gobind Singh's death. Bhai Mani Singh gave it its name, which means 'The Book of the Tenth Master'. Printed copies of the Dasam Granth are identical, and are 1,428 pages long. The most spiritual poems take up about 160 pages. The rest are sometimes secular in their themes. Some may be by other poets at the Guru's court.

One poem called *Jap*, which means 'meditation', is part of the daily prayer of Sikhs. It defines God in terms rather like those of Guru Nanak's *Mul Mantra*, the first words of the Guru Granth Sahib. It begins:

> God has no mark or symbols, no colour or caste, not even family lineage. God's form, hue, shape and dress can be described by no one. God is immovable and self-existent. God shines in no borrowed splendour. No one can measure God's might.
>
> *Jap Sahib* (first hymn): Guru Gobind Singh

In another hymn he says: 'Worship none but God. Do not worship things made by God. Know that God is the one who was from the beginning, the unborn, the invincible, the indestructible' (*Shabad Hazare* number 5). The Guru was a man of great faith, but he knew that almost everything that can be said in attempts to describe God must be negative.

Other verses called *swayyas* (quatrains) from the *Akal Ustat*, which means 'In Praise of the Immortal', are recited at the initiation ceremony.

Guru Gobind Singh's Teachings

In one of his hymns the Guru, who spent much of his life fighting against injustice, spoke of his own birth and the purpose of his life: 'The divine Guru [God] sent me for righteousness' sake. For this purpose I was born; to advance righteousness, set free the good who are oppressed, and destroy evil-doers.' He describes himself as being in God's presence, taking birth at God's command and not because of *karma*, the law of rebirth which requires a person to be reborn as the consequences of deeds performed in a previous life. However, the Guru did not claim divinity. In another of his verses he wrote: 'Recognise all humanity as one. The same Lord is creator and nourisher of all. Recognise no distinction among them.'

?

1 Many of the hymns of Guru Gobind Singh are deeply spiritual, yet he did not include any in the Adi Granth when he added those of his father in 1704. What reasons might he have had for making his decision?

2 What might have been Bhai Mani Singh's reasons for compiling the Dasam Granth in 1734?

Chapter 11

Worship

Worship in the Sikh religion is directed to the transcendent and all-pervading reality called the Akal Purkh (the Timeless Being). It is the Sikh name for God that corresponds to 'the Almighty' in English. 'God the one alone pervades everywhere. As there is none other like him, to whom else are we to make an offering in worship?' said Guru Nanak (Adi Granth 1345).

Simran, or remembrance of God, is the essence of Sikhism, but *simran* without *sewa* (selfless service) often leads to pride. The fusion of the two into one, however, paves the way for self-realisation. The importance and interdependence of these two aspects of spiritual effort is clear from the scriptures: 'True worship consists in the meditation of God's name, for without his name there is no worship' (Adi Granth 489), and 'There can be no worship without performing good deeds' (Adi Granth 4).

Many gurdwaras *encourage young Sikhs to learn musical instruments and lead the singing of* kirtan. *Why?*

Poetry and Music

The whole of the Sikh scriptures is in poetry, and music occupies a place of pride in Sikh worship. *Shabads* (hymns) are sung in a slow and steady tone so that the message is clearly understood by the worshippers. What is important is the *Bani* (revelation); poetry and music are brought in merely to magnify the emotional appeal. The music is neither too austere nor too sensuous. It has a distinct tradition of its own. The singing of hymns to the accompaniment of music is called *kirtan*. It is considered as a means of salvation: 'Day and night sing *kirtan* of God and you will never go into the cycle of transmigration' (Adi Granth 624/1: Guru Arjan).

COMMUNAL WORSHIP

People are social animals. They are influenced by the associates they keep with and the company they move in. It is no secret that in good company one becomes good. Sikhs are daily reminded in their prayers to '*Sad ka sang gurmukh-da-mel*' – seek the company of the saintly and associate with God-awakened souls. Holy people teach and preach truth and purity through personal example and warn the worshippers of the pitfalls and temptations: 'Just as a castor plant imbibes the scent of the adjacent sandalwood, similarly even the fallen are emancipated by the company of the true ones', goes the saying (Adi Granth 861/9: Guru Ram Das).

Guru Nanak emphasised the concept of *sangat* (company) in the attainment of God, and explained *sat sangat* as the assembly where the name of God is treasured and repeated (Adi Granth 72) and which provides opportunities for mutual help. 'Holy congregation is the school of the true guru. There we learn to love God and appreciate his greatness', said Guru Ram Das (Adi Granth 1,316).

The communal worship which has become a characteristic feature of Sikh spirituality is rooted in the practice started by Guru Nanak himself. The Sikh devotees of Guru Nanak living with him in the colony established by him at Kartarpur, and the casual visitors who came to seek his blessings, formed the congregation of his early morning and late evening services. There they sang the hymns composed by Guru Nanak himself and shared a common meal thereafter. Guru Amas Das strengthened the institutions of *sangat* and *langar* (the communal dining: see below) with the appointments of preachers called *sangatias*. Guru Arjan's first installation of the scriptures in the Golden Temple fixed their position at the centre of Sikh worship and life.

Sikh worship in all its forms and its social meaning, however, can be observed fully only in the Sikhs' day-to-day worship in a *gurdwara*.

> Sing his praise, hear it sung and lovingly enshrine it in your heart. He will take you to the abode of peace, destroying all your miseries.
>
> Adi Granth 2

THE GURDWARA

A place set aside by Sikhs for collective meditation and worship is called the *gurdwara*; that is, the House of the Guru. The Guru Granth Sahib, the Holy Scripture of the Sikhs, is their Guru (see Chapter 10), and so a *gurdwara* is a place where the Guru Granth Sahib is installed. The word of God and the holy congregation were the two means employed by the Sikh Gurus for the development of Sikh piety and character, and the *gurdwara* is the place where the two elements are united. Guru Arjan, the compiler of the Sikh scripture, who gave Sikhs a typical design of a *gurdwara* in the form of the present Golden Temple at Amritsar in India, emphasised the importance of such a place in the following words: 'That place alone is holy where one dwells on God. That heart alone is sacred which cherishes the praises of the Lord. That place alone is sanctified where abide men of God' (Adi Granth 107). He went further and said that the 'Holy book is the abode of God' (Adi Granth 1,226/3). It is in this special sense that a *gurdwara* is also called the House of God, though Sikhs believe that God is everywhere.

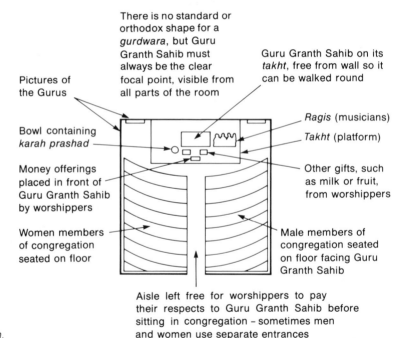

There is no standard or orthodox shape for a *gurdwara*, but Guru Granth Sahib must always be the clear focal point, visible from all parts of the room

Guru Granth Sahib on its *takht*, free from wall so it can be walked round

Pictures of the Gurus

Bowl containing *karah prashad*

Money offerings placed in front of Guru Granth Sahib by worshippers

Women members of congregation seated on floor

Ragis (musicians)

Takht (platform)

Other gifts, such as milk or fruit, from worshippers

Male members of congregation seated on floor facing Guru Granth Sahib

Aisle left free for worshippers to pay their respects to Guru Granth Sahib before sitting in congregation – sometimes men and women use separate entrances

A typical gurdwara *plan.*

HISTORICAL ORIGINS

Sikhs can worship anywhere, even in a tent if the Guru Granth Sahib is installed in it. As a matter of fact, on festive occasions and at special Sikh gatherings, large awnings and tents are pitched in the grounds of *gurdwaras* or in the open spaces nearby for public worship. In the early days of Sikhism, the people who followed the teachings of Guru Nanak and his successors worshipped by singing the Gurus' hymns and talking about the things they did or said. They had no special buildings for worship, but met in each other's homes.

Sikhs outside India do the same even today. They are now scattered all over the world, and it is not always possible to find or build *gurdwaras* everywhere. There are some Sikhs in countries where they are not allowed to build *gurdwaras* even if they can afford to raise the necessary funds for the purpose.

The early Sikhs did not erect special buildings for the simple reason that it would have drawn the attention of the authorities to them, and not all Muslim rulers of the time were sympathetic to non-Muslim places of worship. The humble buildings the Sikhs used for worship and for other social needs of the community were called *dharamsalas* – the places for the practice of *dharma* (righteousness). For Indians this does not just mean worship, it covers the whole of life, so *gurdwaras* are community centres.

During the reign of Akbar in the second half of the sixteenth century, Muslim persecution of Hindu subjects ceased for a while and the Sikhs, who were then still a small minority, started their building programme with the construction of a central place of worship called Harimandir at Amritsar. With the death of Akbar in 1605, the Muslim attitude changed again and the Sikh fortunes suffered a serious set-back. Guru Arjan fell a martyr for the Sikh faith, and the hopes of Sikh ascendancy faded for the time being. Soon after, however, the Sikh religion took a martial turn (see Chapter 3) and the distinctive places of Sikh worship called the *gurdwaras* came into being. The tall Sikh flags, bearing the symbol of the *khanda* (see Chapter 3) and lovingly called the *nishan sahibs* (that is, the 'guru's symbol'), proclaimed the existence of the Sikh communities here and there in the north-west of India in the hostile period of the seventeenth century. These communities were determined to defend their way of life at all costs. Most of the existing beautiful historical buildings, however, were constructed in the second half of the eighteenth century and in the early nineteenth century, when the Sikhs had gained political power in the Punjab.

?

1 The word *gurdwara* can be given at least two meanings besides 'Sikh place of worship'. What are they?
2 Only two things are really necessary for a *gurdwara*. One is a Sikh community. What is the other?
3 How can a *gurdwara* be recognised from the outside?
4 Describe the *nishan sahib*.

Historical Buildings, New Buildings

There are many places associated with the birth of the Sikh Gurus, their visits and some important historical development of the Sikh religion. *Gurdwaras* were often built on these sites, which later on developed into pilgrimage centres in response to such utterances of the Gurus as 'Evergreen is the place where my true Guru lives: those

The Bangla Sahib
gurdwara *in Delhi.*

who saw my true Guru, their souls flowered' (Adi Granth 310), and 'Wherever is my true Guru, blessed, blessed is that place. The devotees search out that sanctuary and apply the sacred dust of its precincts to their faces' (Adi Granth 450).

Many of these historical *gurdwaras* are being rebuilt, with extensive use of marble for embellishment and durability. Old architectural features have given way to concrete. Calligraphy and mirror-work have taken the place of detailed fresco and plaster decoration, destroying much of the historical evidence in the process. The characteristic eye-catching white dome, sometimes gilded, and the typical smaller cupolas on the corners and row of turrets on the parapet, which lend these *gurdwaras* an air of individuality and distinctiveness peculiar to Sikh religious buildings, have been retained to keep to the tradition. Outside India – for instance, in the United Kingdom – these few features have been dispensed with, even in the case of purpose-built *gurdwaras*. The *nishan sahib* is often the only visible Sikh symbol, but this pinpoints a Sikh place of worship even when the services are held in an ordinary house converted into a *gurdwara*, or when a redundant Christian church is acquired for worship.

THE GURDWARA OFFICIALS

When a *gurdwara* is established, the first thing the community has to do is to appoint someone to look after it. Sikhism has no priesthood, hereditary or professional. In village *gurdwaras*, where most of the Sikh population is based, the community will appoint a man who can recite the scriptures, sing hymns and perform religious rites. He is respectfully called *Bhaiji* (Brother). The ceremonial work is not his

The Guru Granth Sahib being carried to its resting place at the end of the day.

exclusive task, but is shared by other members of the community. His most important duty, however, is to get up early in the morning and arrange the morning service. He will strike the gong to announce that service will commence shortly, so that the people who would like to join him should come to the *gurdwara* immediately. In the evening a short service is also held before closing the scripture for the night.

Such an official could be a part-time worker or a volunteer free to do any other job during the day. But when a full-time *granthi* (the reader of the scriptures and caretaker of the building) is taken on, then he is provided with free board and lodging along with some cash payment.

The Management Committee

A *gurdwara* is managed by a committee chosen or elected by the congregation, usually every year or two years. The members of the committee are *gurdwara* employees who are responsible to the congregation for their activities and accounts. No outside religious organisation is involved or has supervisory powers over them. The office bearers are not paid, but their position gives them prestige in the community.

Services and Celebrations

In big towns and cities the *gurdwara* staff have always enough work on their hands, though of a fairly routine nature. Apart from the daily morning and evening fixed services, there are occasional and special public functions which keep them fully occupied.

Regular services on Sangrand, the first day of every solar month of the Indian calendar, are held in the *gurdwaras*. They serve both a practical and a religious need. People, despite the popularity of the Gregorian (modern Western) calendar, still use the Indian calendar for counting days and for religious festivities. There is a hymn in the Guru Granth Sahib covering the twelve months of the year, and a section is read each month. The spiritual message conveyed through this has a value of its own.

The celebrations linked with birth anniversaries of the Gurus during the year, which last for three days, involve a good deal of planning and physical work for the *granthis* and committees. In addition, very often full readings of the scriptures are commissioned by individual Sikhs on the eve of the marriage of their children, on the successful completion of a venture, on the recovery of a dear one from illness, on the birth of a son, to mark the close of a death ceremony, etc. These full readings take about 48 hours. Solemnisation of weddings and performance of funeral services also call for the time of the *gurdwara* staff. All these social-cum-religious functions, whether they are arranged in the homes or at the *gurdwaras*, require the guidance and participation of the *gurdwara* officials and committee members.

Other Functions

A *gurdwara* is primarily a place of worship and people flock there to find spiritual solace from everyday woes and worries, and to seek a way to peace and purity. But that does not prevent the use of the premises for purely secular and social purposes. Outside India, marriages are solemnised in the *gurdwaras*, partly because of legal requirements, and partly owing to the availability of facilities for cooking for many guests. The place is also used for the teaching of Punjabi – the language of Sikh scripture and worship – and the rudiments of Sikh religion and culture to children. Room is kept for lodging travellers and newly arrived immigrants. In Britain most Sikh women go out to work and elderly Sikhs, both men and women, can feel lonely and bored at home. Many *gurdwaras* have opened day centres for them in recent years.

Comforting the sick and dying in hospitals, consoling bereaved families in their homes, counselling couples whose marriages are in danger of breaking up, gaining *gurdwara* support for widows and orphans, securing work for the unemployed and the handicapped and speaking at public meetings do not strictly form part of the work entrusted to the care of the *granthi*. These are the responsibility of the community at large, or at least of the caste kinship groups (see Chapter 17). But on the whole such vital needs of the community go unattended to or neglected if it is not someone's particular duty, so in the West the *granthi* often takes on these functions.

Staff Behaviour

One thing which is rated very highly among Sikhs is the standard of behaviour expected of the employees of a *gurdwara*. Their private and public lives are always under the close scrutiny of the community. A slight suspicion of a moral lapse on their part can throw them out of employment. Betting, gambling or drinking are not the pastimes meant for them. A vow of celibacy is not regarded as a sure passport to immaculate behaviour. A family man, preferably middle-aged, is generally considered suitable to hold the office of *granthi*. The tenure of his office will last as long as he can maintain a high moral character and can steer clear of the *gurdwara's* internal politics.

1 What work does a *granthi* do in a *gurdwara*?
2 What other name might he be called?
3 What qualities should he possess?

TIMES OF WORSHIP

The *gurdwara* is not a place which opens at fixed hours of the day only. In India it is kept open from dawn to dusk every day of the week for devotees and visitors alike. People who can find time participate in the morning and evening services. Others just pop in and kneel before the scripture, sit there for a while and listen if someone is reading it. Some will read a few pages themselves, or just a lesson for the day.

It has also become an established practice at many places for women to have a gathering of their own in the *gurdwara* once a week, often in the afternoon. Sikhs are, however, under no religious or customary command to meet for special congregational worship on any particular day of the week in addition to the normal daily services, as Christians do on Sundays and Muslims do on Fridays. In a town or a district with more than one *gurdwara*, the special services (called *diwan*) are held on different days of the week to attract more people. The weekday services take place in the evening and last for two to three hours. Sunday, being a public holiday, attracts the largest number of worshippers everywhere, and the services then are much longer.

All the *gurdwaras* provide the same type of religious service and facilities to the community and the people attend one or the other, according to their convenience and the attractiveness of the service on a particular day. The different names given to the *gurdwara*, such as the Singh Sabha Gurdwara, the Ramgarhia Sikh Gurdwara, Singh Sabha Bhatra Gurdwara or simply the Sikh Temple, do not reflect doctrinal difference among the Sikhs. They show which one of the various cultural groups within the larger Sikh community has established a particular *gurdwara*, and is dominant in its managing committee.

THE CONGREGATION

The whole family, including small children, go to the *gurdwara* in their Sunday best. The interior of the *gurdwara* is generally bare, except for a few portraits of the Gurus fixed on the wall behind the Guru Granth Sahib. On festive occasions the *diwan* hall is sometimes decorated with coloured buntings, streamers and lights.

Before entering the assembly hall, the worshippers take off their shoes and leave them outside in the cloakroom or to be looked after by volunteers. Once inside the *gurdwara*, everybody, Sikh or not, is required to cover his or her head. For non-Sikh visitors square pieces of cloth are kept ready for use. Tobacco is taboo for the Sikhs and visitors are reminded not to keep it on their persons when visiting a *gurdwara*. Any person under the influence of alcohol will also be requested to leave the premises.

Within the *gurdwara*, the first and most important act to be observed by Sikhs is to approach the Guru Granth Sahib reverentially with their offerings of money, flowers or food for the *gurdwara* kitchen, and bow or prostrate themselves in front of it until their foreheads touch the ground. Standing up, they will move back, but without turning their backs upon the scripture, and sit in the congregation. There are no chairs or benches; all sit on the floor, which is covered with mats or carpets. No distinctions, either to highlight religious or social status or between Sikhs and non-Sikhs, are allowed in the matter of seating arrangements.

Men and women worship together, though sitting separately. Tradition does not allow a free mixing of the sexes in any walk of life; in the *gurdwara*, for reasons of traditional modesty and to avoid embarrassment to them, the women are left to themselves. In the absence of creches and play areas, it usually falls upon the women to keep the children calm and contented during the long hours of the service. Sikh women, however, do not veil themselves when sitting in the congregation and are free to sing or speak to the worshippers.

Distributing karah prashad.

1 In India *gurdwaras* are usually open from before dawn until after nightfall. Why do some in Britain only open on Sundays or in the evening?

2 **a** How do Sikhs show respect for the Guru Granth Sahib when they enter the room where it is kept?

   b What will they have done immediately before entering the room?

   c Why do you think worshippers sit on the floor rather than on chairs?

   d Why do men and women usually sit separately in the *gurdwara*?

THE SERVICE

Sikh congregational worship includes the reading of the scriptures and the singing of *shabads* (hymns) from Guru Granth Sahib and other approved Sikh works, such as the compositions of Guru Gobind Singh and passages from the writings of Bhai Gurdas and Bhai Nand Lal. Worshippers also listen to explanations of the scriptural passages, to emphasise moral virtues or clarify ideological tangles; and to lectures or addresses on the current problems faced by the Sikh community, both at home and abroad.

The First Lesson and Hymns

The service begins usually at daybreak: the *granthi* opens the Guru Granth Sahib and reads the lesson from it. Sikhs call it *Vak laina*. The Guru Granth Sahib is opened at random and the first passage on the left-hand page is read. Sometimes it may be necessary to turn back to the beginning on the previous page. This is regarded as the Guru's guidance for the day. In some *gurdwaras* the *Vak* is posted on the noticeboard for the information of the people who come to the *gurdwara* later in the day. The recitation of the scripture continues till the *granthi* finds that enough people have arrived in the *gurdwara*, when *kirtan* (hymn singing) should begin. There is, however, no fixed schedule, nor is a certain number of people needed before the service can begin.

Asa di-Var, a favourite composition of Guru Nanak, forms the prelude to the *kirtan* session. It touches on several spiritual and moral truths and the *ragis* (musicians) will add to it with songs of praise, requests for spiritual guidance and thanks for human birth and sustenance. Selections of hymns are always available in the *gurdwaras* but the worshippers prefer to listen and seldom join in the singing, even when they know the text.

The elderly and people who do not have domestic duties to perform make their way to the gurdwara to listen to the early devotional music, marked by its serenity and peacefulness. With the arrival of the families the atmosphere becomes more informal and relaxed. People come and go all the time. While entering and leaving, they may be seen talking to one another and the children may quietly leave their mothers and play among the worshippers. It then becomes the most unpleasant duty of the community leader or the secretary of the management committee to ask the congregation to be quiet and attentive!

The Exposition and the Address

Kirtan is followed by *katha*, an explanation of a hymn chosen by the speaker. He may begin by reciting the passage in full and then explain it line by line, illustrating it with proverbs and anecdotes from the lives of the Gurus and the Sikhs. Examples may be drawn from other religions as well, but not with the intention of denigrating them.

Giving a lecture in a Leeds gurdwara.

To keep the congregation well informed about the day-to-day social and political problems faced by the Sikh community is also an important aspect of the congregational gatherings. A speaker may begin the address like this: '*Waheguru ji ka Khalsa, waheguru ji ke fateh*' (The Khalsa belongs to God. Victory belongs to God). Then he will speak to them about the matter of concern – a racial attack or whatever it might be. Discussing political problems is not out of bounds in the *gurdwaras*, but a spiritual atmosphere must be preserved while so doing.

Outside India it is not unusual to squeeze a wedding ceremony into the regular weekly worship. People who are not interested leave for the community kitchen (*langar* – see below), which is kept open during the service, and come back for the final act of worship if it is still on. When nothing else is left to be done then people will stand for *ardas*.

The Petition

Ardas forms the core of a set of hymns for the epilogue of the service. It takes about a quarter of an hour and is said standing. *Ardas* literally means 'a petition'. It invokes the blessings of God and the Gurus before recalling the sacrifices made by Sikh men and women for the preservation of the Sikh faith and its traditions. It seeks God's forgiveness for any transgressions committed by individuals and by the community as a whole. It prays for the grace of God and for enlightenment to lead a virtuous life. It concludes with a prayer for the welfare of humanity as a whole.

Sharing Food

With the reading of a final lesson from the Guru Granth Sahib, followed by the distribution of *karah prashad*, the congregation breaks up to partake of a meal called *langar* in the common kitchen, which is attached to the *gurdwara*. A small helping of *karah prashad* – a cooked mixture of flour, sugar and clarified butter – is distributed. People eat this together to remind them that they are equal and members of one community. The *langar*, which is a full, communal vegetarian meal, is meant for strengthening community solidarity and breaking down caste barriers peculiar to Indian society (see Chapter 17).

1 Describe Sikh worship, using and explaining the words *shabad*, *kirtan*, and *katha*.
2 a What is *karah prashad*?
  b How is it made? (Perhaps you could make some yourself.)
  c What is the significance of *karah prashad*?
  d Why would Sikhs be upset if a visitor refused to eat it?
3 a What is *langar*?
  b Why is only vegetarian food served at *langar*?
  c *Langar* is always a part of worship and many other rituals. One reason for its importance is Sikh hospitality. What others can you suggest?

SYMBOLS

The centrality of the scripture in a *gurdwara* is quite obvious to everybody, and to be expected, but a visitor might be surprised to find swords and arrows placed on the dais in front of the Guru Granth Sahib, and to see the *karah prashad* touched with a sword before it is distributed. The flag outside the *gurdwara*, too, bears the symbol of *khanda* (see Chapter 3), and in some *gurdwaras* a kettle-drum is beaten in a martial style to announce the conclusion of a service and the invitation to a meal in the *gurdwara*. The weapons of war and their association with certain acts of worship and ceremonies, such as *amrit*-taking, symbolise the Sikh insistence that the use of force is not immoral in all circumstances. People should not lose courage when their very existence and their natural rights are threatened, but should defend themselves with the weapons at their command. The message is 'Do not shrink to face the danger, but go armed.' A Sikh is a *sant sipahi* (a saint-soldier), a person of piety and, when challenged, a fighter rolled into one. A sword is a constant companion of an initiated Sikh.

1 Give as many reasons as you can to explain why congregational worship is important to Sikhs.
2 Imagine an aunt comes from India to visit Sikh relatives in Britain. What might surprise her when she went to a British *gurdwara*? (Some clues are: architecture, Sunday, school, wedding.) How might her relatives explain the differences?

Chapter 12	# *The Idea of God and of Humanity*

The idea of God is practically universal throughout the human race. We learn of God first by hearsay, for we are born into a world where God's name is in constant use.

> You are clearly present in the world, O Lord,
> Because all crave for your name,

> Adi Granth 71/25

the Sikh teaching declares. No belief about the nature of God and creation, however, can be proved intellectually or demonstrated scientifically. Experience alone has kept both saints and scholars occupied in unravelling this enigma, ever since the speculation began.

THE SIKH CONCEPT OF GOD

Religious doctrines and creeds about the existence, nature and relation of God and humanity, worked out by saints and scholars on the basis of their own limited experiences, have many things unexplained and unaccounted for: 'He who tastes it alone knows its taste. It is like the dumb tasting the sweet' (Adi Granth 608/1). That 'the attributes of God cannot be comprehended and without actually seeing him one cannot describe him adequately' (Adi Granth 1,256) may seem obvious, but this has not put off theologians from asserting and justifying their claims with rigidity and stubbornness. The futility of such an exercise has aptly been described by Guru Nanak in the following hymn in the Guru Granth Sahib:

> No one has found your worth. Everyone narrates your glory as he has repeatedly heard. Spiritual guides, prophets, divine preceptors, men of faith, virtuous men, martyrs, preachers, obtain more blessings if they continue reading God's praises. He consults none when he builds nor does he consult anyone when he demolishes; while giving and taking he seeks the counsel of none. His omnipotence he himself knows and he himself does all the works. How great is the place where my sovereign resides. No one can reach it, to whom should I go to ask?

> Adi Granth 53

Although people cannot comprehend God, it does not mean that we can have no knowledge of God at all. It is true that no decisive proof of God's existence can be found to refute the ingenious arguments put forward by atheists and agnostics. It is equally true that many honest and intellectual people have wrestled with the problem and have come out with a plain 'yes', but it still, however, remains a question of faith. As Guru Arjan said:

> He who believes in God as truth in his heart
> Shall see him as the root of everything.
> He who in his heart is truly convinced of the existence of God
> Has his mind illumined by true knowledge.
>
> Adi Granth 285/12

Sikhs believe a person of faith has something to hold on to, a mooring point, or a destination to reach and there rest: 'Whosoever sees God's omnipotence with his eyes, hears the Word with his ears, and utters the name with his mouth, he obtains the full wealth of honours and his attention is easily fixed on God' (Adi Granth 1,168/8: Guru Nanak). Guru Nanak also said:

> The Lord, who creating the world pervades it, is known through his nature. Seek not the True One somewhere far away, recognise the Word [Divine Spirit] dwelling in every heart. Recognise the True One, the Word [His will], and do not think the one who created this universe to be far away. Peace comes from contemplating the name alone; without realising the name [of God] the game of life remains incomplete.
>
> Adi Granth 581/6

?   How does a Sikh find faith in God helpful?

THE MUL MANTRA

ਜਪੁ ਜੀ ਸਾਹਿਬ

The Mul Mantra, which forms the first words of the Guru Granth Sahib.

Guru Nanak knew the differing religions found in the India of his day. The scriptural knowledge which he acquired from Hindu and Muslim teachers was added to by his visiting the places of pilgrimage and religious fairs which are a characteristic feature of Indian spirituality, and talking to priests, teachers and gurus. Guru Nanak's understanding of God could therefore be attributed to his close familiarity with this vast storehouse of doctrines and dogmas as perceived through his own spiritual insights. His statement of this understanding reads:

> There is one God. Eternal truth is his name, creator of all things, and the all-pervading spirit. Fearless and without hatred, timeless and formless. Beyond birth and death, self-enlightened. By the grace of the Guru he is known.
>
> Adi Granth 1, the *Mul Mantra*

It would be wrong to claim that these words give us a total idea of God. They are not intended to do so. They simply give the Sikh view of God, by describing the main attributes of God.

'MY GOD IS ONE'

Sikhism is strictly a monotheistic faith. This means that God is the one eternal Being, the one and sole reality in the cosmos to whom worship should be offered. This supreme Being exists of itself, has not become itself. It simply is. It is without beginning and without end. The morning prayer of the Sikhs opens with such an affirmation:

> The True One was in the beginning.
> The True One was before all ages began.
> The True One is also.
> Nanak says the True One shall ever be.   Adi Granth 1

Belief in the unity and uniqueness of God has been repeatedly emphasised by such verses as 'My God is one, brethren, my God is one' (Adi Granth 350), and 'This alone is his merit, that there is none other like him' (Adi Granth 349). Such statements as 'God is without a second, and no one equals him' (Adi Granth 597) look quite simple on the surface, yet contain deep meanings and wide implications.

GOD AS CREATOR

God is the creator of everything known and unknown. The universe is not therefore to be regarded as something self-perpetuating and automatic. Whatever exists is believed to receive existence from God. How and when this universe came to exist is known to God alone: 'When God so willed the universe came into being' (Adi Granth 1,036). A Sikh would not take literally the various descriptions of creation given in the scriptures. The Sikh Gurus picked them up either to refute them or just to use them as props while driving home some important spiritual or moral truths, without in any way granting the descriptions' authenticity or acceptance. What emerges out of these conflations is that God alone is the creator, sustainer and destroyer of this manifest world: 'God is both the efficient and material cause of everything' (Adi Granth 288/4).

Immanence and Transcendence

God is immanent – that is, he is everywhere and in everything – and there seems to be, therefore, no contradiction in saying that everything is in God: 'God created himself and assumed a name. Second besides himself he created nature. Seated in nature he watches with delight what he creates' (Adi Granth 463).

Does it make any difference if we call him transcendent (above and beyond creation) or immanent? He is both. How can the created know the limits of the creator and pass judgements? There is no conception in Sikhism of a creator who sits apart from his creation.

Attitudes to Images and Incarnation

A characteristic and comprehensive view of Sikh thinking on the subject is available in the following hymn of Guru Nanak:

Unknowable, infinite, unapproachable and imperceptible is my Lord. He is not subject to death and destiny. His caste is castelessness. He is unborn, self-illuminated and without desire and doubt. He has no form, no colour, and no features and is revealed only through the True Word. He has neither father, nor mother, nor sons, nor kindred, nor wife. You, O Lord, are without ancestry, immaculate, transcendent and infinite. Your light pervades all.

Adi Granth 597

Why do you think there are no pictures or statues inside this gurdwara?

Thus creation cannot be equated with the creator and cannot, therefore, take its place for worship. Bowing before idols and images is forbidden for the simple reason that they are human handiwork, and therefore twice removed from the unseen, ultimate reality. That is why teachings against idolatry are so strong. As Guru Arjan said:

> He who thinks that stone is God
> Worships in vain.
> He who prostrates before stones
> Labours to no purpose.

Adi Granth 1,160

Sikhism also rejects the view that God ever assumes any physical form, either animal or human. Guru Arjan emphatically denounced it by saying: 'May the mouth burn by which it is said that the Lord becomes incarnate. He neither comes to nor departs from this earth. The God of Nanak is all-absorbing and ever-present' (Adi Granth 1,136).

A PERSONAL GOD

The Sikh Gurus believed in a personal God who could be worshipped and loved. They always addressed God in personal language. For instance:

> Without thee, O my Lord, I know not any other.
> I ever sing thine praises.

Adi Granth 795: Guru Nanak

O, Lord, we are sinners.
We seek the refuge of thy door.

Adi Granth 167: Guru Amar Das

You are the Lord, we pray to you.

Adi Granth 268: Guru Arjan

For a Sikh, God is not only transcendent but immanent also: 'God is hidden in every heart and every heart is illumined by him' (Adi Granth 597). The Sikh feels God's presence within and turns towards this person, Sat Purkh (the in-dwelling spirit), when he prays: 'The True One is not far from us, but resides within us' (Adi Granth 421/4).

Throughout their poetic revelations the Gurus emphasise repeatedly that God himself is directly available to everyone, as parents are to their children: 'The One God is the Father of all. We are all his children' (Adi Granth 611). We can therefore all communicate with God direct.

'The Formless One'

The object of concentration is neither an image nor any physical being. It is the abstract, timeless, eternal reality (Akal Purkh). The intensity of devotion sometimes bursts forth in such ecstatic utterances as this: 'Beauteous are the Lord's eyes, sparkling his teeth, graceful is thy gait, O Lord, sweet thy speech' (Adi Granth 567/10), which nearly verge on idolatry. Such expressions, however, are to be taken figuratively. They are a concession to human inability to describe the experience otherwise; but no person is God, nor is God a person. Guru Nanak never taught that God is just an enlargement of man. On the contrary, a concept such as '*nirankar*' ('formless') emphasises the supra-human dimension of God: 'Your name, O God, is the Formless One. By dwelling on it one does not go to hell' (Adi Granth 465).

1 What does a Sikh mean by saying that God is personal?
2 Some Sikhs are not very happy to use the word 'personal' because they think it might be misunderstood. What reasons can you suggest for their anxieties?

NAMES FOR GOD

It is immaterial what pronouns we use for God, whether 'he', 'she' or 'it'. For a person of faith, God is everything. What matters is not the thing but its essence. Guru Nanak at one place writes that: 'You yourself are the male and yourself the female. You yourself are the chessboard [the world] and yourself the chessman [the human being]' (Adi Granth 1,020). At another place he clarifies further the nature of its essence by saying that: 'The wise and beauteous God is neither a woman, nor a man, nor a bird' (Adi Granth 1,010). Thus God can be addressed in any manner, by any name and in any language, so long as the essence of the terms used means 'One Almighty God' and not any human being or objects of this world.

'Your names are countless, O Lord. I do not know their end, but of one thing I am sure; that there is not another like you', said Guru Nanak (Adi Granth 877). The Sikh Gurus and the saints whose works have been included in the Sikh scriptures have used a large number of names to describe God which were current among the Hindus and Muslims. Guru Gobind Singh's *Jap* (devotional song) contains about 950 names and epithets for God, bringing out his diverse attributes, positive as well as negative. The Sikh Gurus, however, preferred to call God 'Satnam' – the eternal reality. God is called Satnam in the *Mul Mantra*, which begins the Guru Granth Sahib. Elsewhere the word is repeatedly emphasised. Two examples are 'O my mind, meditate on the Sat [the true one] Sada Sat, the eternally true' (Adi Granth 1,201/22: Guru Ram Das), and 'My tongue utters God's attributive names. "Satnam" is his primal and traditional name' (Adi Granth 1,083: Guru Arjan). '*Waheguru*' (the wonderful Lord) has also become popular among the Sikhs.

1   List the names which are used for God in this section and try to explain each one.
2   'Truth' or the 'True Name' are very important names of God. Try to explain why they are so significant.

THE SIKH CONCEPT OF HUMANITY

Humanity regards itself as the crown of creation, and people think that they understand a good deal about their creator. Whether the body is 'formed of the slime of the earth' or is composed of the five primal elements (Adi Granth 1,426) – earth, water, fire, air and space – it derives its vitality from the breath of life which God breathed into its face. Human indebtedness to God is acknowledged by exclamations such as 'O my body, God infused his light in you and you were born in the world' (Adi Granth 921/18).

THE SOUL

The mysterious constituent which accounts for the body's being alive is called the soul. Sikhism shares the belief, common among the religions of Indian origin, that 'the soul neither dies nor can it be destroyed' (Adi Granth 1,026/1), and that it survives after death. Body and soul, however, are complementary to each other; one cannot do without the other:

> The beautiful mansion, the body, is the Temple of God. In it he has installed his light infinite.
>
> Adi Granth 1,256

> In the pure body is the spotless swan [soul] and within it is *nam* [the Divine Spirit], an emanation from the pure one.
>
> Adi Granth 1,034/22

Man, you are an image of light, recognise your essence.

Adi Granth 441/4

The spirit that illumines the human soul, however, equally sustains all other beings. All creatures have been given consciousness: 'None has been created without it. They follow the path according to their understanding, and judged in the same way they come and go' (Adi Granth 24/27).

But it seems that God has endowed humanity with superior understanding and reason, with the capacity to exploit natural resources to its advantage and improve its own life and environment.

THE SENSE OF RIGHT AND WRONG

People are moral beings. They are value conscious. Their moral and spiritual guide is within them: 'Creating man and infusing in him his spirit, the Lord set it as a judge in his conscience' (Adi Granth 463/23). This innate sense of discrimination enables people to distinguish right from wrong. Sometimes, though, under the impact of outside influences, such as heredity, environment, bad friends and habits, this judgement is impaired and the stirrings of conscience go unheeded. The very realisation of a wrong action or harm done to someone else deliberately or accidentally, however, makes one feel ashamed and crestfallen, while a good deed makes one feel happy and proud. 'The two tendencies of right and wrong are written in the destiny of man. Through these he sows the seeds of virtue and vice' (Adi Granth 1,038/10). Ethical conduct and social righteousness emanate from this latent power of self-reflection.

Natural and Moral Laws

Humanity is the apex of creation, but people are conscious of their limitations as well. Humanity has not created itself and cannot keep itself alive forever: 'God sends us and we take birth. He calls us back and we die' (Adi Granth 1,239). Our stay in the world is uncertain because 'we do not know the span of our life and time of our death' (Adi Granth 660).

So people are free to do whatever they like, but only within the framework of natural and moral laws. The transgression of these, knowingly or in ignorance, causes pain and unhappiness. The more we know about them, the greater our freedom to act. We feel unhappy when our efforts do not bear the desired fruit or our ambitions are thwarted by something unseen and unexpected. It remains for us a profound and impenetrable mystery. This is the human predicament. 'No man lives long enough to exhaust his wishes and accomplish his task' (Adi Granth 1,412). But why is it so? The answer could be 'because God has made it so': as the scripture says, 'All that happens is in his will and there is not another who does a thing' (Adi Granth 154/1).

SUFFERING AND GOD'S LAWS

Suffering is the common lot of all human beings: 'From the beginning of time, pain and pleasure are written in man's fate by the creator' (Adi Granth 1,054/18). People strive hard for self-preservation, happiness and peace; try to build up defences against natural disasters; devise ways and means to combat the treachery of fellow humans; formulate programmes for the eradication of social evils, and establish centres for medical research. The successes achieved in these areas are praiseworthy, but a sense of security and the comforts of life have not been able to provide mental satisfaction to everyone: 'Man is afflicted by ego and *maya* [worldly attachments], so he suffers' (Adi Granth 352/22).

Scriptures show us the way to wean away the mind from the evil influence of ego and *maya*. *Sewa* (selfless service) and *simran* (remembrance of God) purify the mind and inculcate charity for all. They bring about moral and spiritual transformation in the life of individuals. Such people are concerned with their own efforts and not with the outcome of their actions. Success or failure have no meaning for one who believes that everything happens according to God's laws. After this realisation, God-oriented people live in a natural state of perfect calm and composure: 'By submission to your will all my pains are turned into pleasure. Through the name of the True One all my sufferings have ended' (Adi Granth 412/13).

?

1   What are the five primal elements from which everything is made?
2   According to Sikh belief, in what ways are human beings different from other animals?
3   **a**   What is the cause of suffering, according to Sikh teaching?
     b   How can suffering be overcome?

DUTY TO OTHERS

The Sikh religion stands for a God-centred righteous life in the midst of normal worldly activities. This ideal cannot be better stated than in the following words of Guru Arjan: 'the highest of all religions is to meditate on God and live a pure life' (Adi Granth 266/19). The spiritual standing of a man or woman has no meaning if he or she fails to guide the naive and ignorant towards a meaningful life of truth. The Sikh assertion that 'The God-conscious man achieves the goal and makes all other do so' (Adi Granth 295) is indicative of the duty of an enlightened person to help those lagging behind on the road of spirituality.

> Man may perform lip-service, austerities and exercise self-restraint, and dwell at places of pilgrimage, but what does it avail him without the True Being. As he sows, so does he reap ... without virtue the human life passes away in vain.
>
> Adi Granth 56/12: Guru Nanak

God-Realisation, Prayer and Meditation

Religion is not merely the learning of religious teachings or the mechanical reading of scriptures and the performance of rites and rituals. It is a disciplined practice of truth which brings about a change of one's character and outlook on life. It is the replacement of ignorance by knowledge or awareness. The end-product of such a spiritual attainment is called enlightenment or self-realisation. 'On knowing the self, man meets God' (Adi Granth 1,410).

Such a person feels at home in the world and enjoys mental and spiritual balance. Such a person's transformed will and changed heart result in complete renewing of his or her nature. This is called second birth or the state of being reborn.

Becoming Reborn

How are we to attain this reborn state? The answer is that we must die in order to live. The change involves a break with the past. 'Being self-centred we die. Becoming God-centred we live' (Adi Granth 1,238). The way to perfection is steep and hard, but nevertheless the goal is always clearly in sight.

A sant *is a spiritually enlightened person who helps others develop their spirituality. Bowing to touch his feet is a sign of respect.*

The first step is constant communion with God through meditating on his attributes. 'Man becomes like the one he serves' (Adi Granth 224), but the decision is left to us to make. There are only two ways, the path of egoism with its love of self, and the path of devotion with its love of God. We have to choose one of them. The former leads to evil and unhappiness and the latter to virtue and contentment: 'those who love God become pure, they give up lust, anger and egoism' (Adi Granth 58). But to get into the habit of

76

centring the mind on God is not easy. It is always better to take advice. 'Even if you can swim in water, learn the art of swimming from those experienced who have faced whirlpools' said Guru Nanak (Adi Granth 1,410). Scriptures are handy for one who desires to consult them: 'When the lamp is lit darkness is dispelled. Similarly by reading the religious books the sinful intellect is destroyed' (Adi Granth 791).

The second step is self-improvement through uprightness of character. The learning of scriptures alone is not enough to know the truth. 'No one is purified without following the path of truthful living', says Guru Nanak (Adi Granth 946), and so what is learnt from the scriptures needs to be put into practice. Whatever deeds we do, we get the fruits of them. 'If we are to get paid for our actions, good or bad, then why engage in sinful deeds?' asked Guru Nanak (Adi Granth 474).

Human beings are a mixture of contradictory and conflicting elements which call for reconciliation. They are capable of extreme goodness and terrible crimes as well, because they are 'full of vice though virtues are also there' (Adi Granth 936). So there is no easy solution. We can overcome temptations only by disciplined effort, and constant struggle is needed to conquer individual weaknesses. Here is the formula put forward by Guru Arjan, if only we could adhere to it: 'Do not delay in practising righteousness, but think before committing an evil. Hold fast to God, and forsake greed. Seek protection of godly people to wash off sins, to become righteous' (Adi Granth 1,354).

Suffering and Resignation

Suffering is another factor that needs explaining. Suffering caused by the death of a dear one, by the loss of hard-earned income, by illness, by political, social, religious or racial discrimination, for example, are at least understandable. We can find ways and means to cope with them or get rid of them; but there are sufferings and calamities over which we have no control at all.

We desire and strive for happiness, but it eludes us – why? It is God's will. We have to reconcile ourselves to this tragic fact of life and submit to it willingly and cheerfully. Guru Nanak in the following hymn describes human helplessness:

> Absurd is the request to ask for the gift of joy and the withdrawal of sorrow. Pleasures and pains are the two garments given to man from the Lord's court. Where one is bound to lose by speech, it is better to be silent.

> Adi Granth 149

Accepting the will of God, therefore, is the only alternative left to us.

When one's attitude to a situation changes, so does the whole situation. Here is the picture of a man that emerges out of a disciplined spiritual endeavour:

He who in adversity grieves not,
He who is without fear;
He who falls not in the snares of sensuality,
Who has no greed for gold, knowing it is like dust;
He who does not slander people when their backs are turned, nor flatter them to their faces;
He who has neither gluttony in his heart, nor vanity, nor attachment to worldly things;
He whom nothing moves, neither good fortune nor ill,
Who cares not for the world's applause nor its censure,
Who ignores every wishful fantasy and accepts what comes his way as it comes;
He whom lust cannot lure, nor anger command;
In such a one lives God himself. On such a man does God's grace descend,
For he knows the righteous path.
O Nanak, his soul mingles with the Lord as water mingles with water.

Adi Granth 633: Guru Teg Bahadur translated by Khushwant Singh

1 What does the phrase 'God-realisation' mean?
2 Sikhs teach that 'we must die in order to live'.
   a What kind of things have to be killed off before God-realisation can happen?
   b Why have people to rid themselves of them?
3 Discuss what you think Guru Nanak meant by saying 'Man becomes like the one he serves' (Adi Granth 224). It refers to women as well as men.
4 Giving things up is only part of the process of God-realisation. What positive steps must a Sikh take?
5 What kinds of values should a God-realised person have? How should he or she relate to God and other human beings?
6 The ninth Guru, Teg Bahadur, described the person who had achieved God-realisation in poetry (Adi Granth 633, quoted in the last paragraph of this section). Try to put what he said into everyday language.

PRAYER

Prayer means the uttering or expression of earnest entreaties. It also means the recitation of prescribed passages from the scriptures at a given time, alone or in unison with others. For someone of faith, the reality of God is a living presence and the act of prayer is the instrument for constant communion with the Unseen Reality. To a God-awakened soul, 'forgetting God even for an instant is a great affliction of the mind' (Adi Granth 21). Prayer is the medium, the way that enables us to expose ourselves fully to the presence and power of God. God does not need our prayers. He does not grow greater by our praise nor does he become less if we ignore him. It is our moral duty, however, to be thankful to God for giving us an exalted position in his creation, and providing us with sustenance and the comforts of life. Guru Arjan rightly leads us to pray, to acknowledge our dependence upon God, in the following words: 'Call upon God with

Offering prayers (ardas *at the start of the* amrit *ceremony.*)

every breath, who has made you high in the range of all creation. This invaluable stage of existence is attained through grace. You must offer all your love' (Adi Granth 270/3).

We should approach God with a pure heart and humble voice and seek his blessings for a successful culmination of our plans and programmes. Utterances such as 'If you desire success in your undertaking then pray to God' (Adi Granth 91) are not a substitute for work, but they are an assurance that inspires courage and resolve to do our best. A Sikh would arrange prayers on all important occasions such as before moving into a new house, starting a new business or going on a long journey. The Sikhs' staunch faith in God's providence and the confidence that 'God can set right what had gone wrong' makes them 'stand and pray before him' (Adi Granth 1,093/8). Prayer does not reduce our will to tackle and solve our problems. We ask God for help and guidance only, and do not unload our problems onto him to solve them for us.

It is not the size or content of the prayer that matters. It is the intention behind it. A Sikh just before starting the car may say 'O God, help me to travel safely'; or a line or two from the scriptures, such as 'He, the Lord, is the only giver. He gives to all, and without limit, for limitless are his treasures' (Adi Granth 257/9), may be recited from memory by way of saying grace before or after meals.

Answers to Prayer

There is nothing wrong in praying for material blessings. People do pray and ask for the fulfilment of their specific desires occasionally. The *Japji*, the daily morning recital of a practising Sikh, however, makes it clear that 'God himself knows our needs and bestows accordingly' (Adi Granth 5). A further reading of the scripture assures us that 'If the seeker cries out and begs at the Lord's door, the Lord hears him, and whether he accepts his petition or rejects it, it is all for his good' (Adi Granth 349/12). The following two citations from the Guru Granth Sahib should suffice to bring home to every one of us that life is governed by certain moral laws and our wishful thinking cannot bend them to our advantage: 'Prayers are offered for material gains but these come to one as is the writ of one's *karma*

(Adi Granth 937/9), and 'All beings are beggars at your door, and you give as is right in your own view' (Adi Granth 504/2).

We do sometimes come across individuals who assert that they prayed to God for a certain gift and they got it. It could be just a coincidence or a miracle, but such things do not happen every day. The very fact of our praying for more may, perhaps, remind us that whatever the earthly gifts we already have, they have come to us through God's grace, and this may prompt us to share them with those who have less.

Prayer is not a magic spell to force God to do our will or to compel God to avert a natural disaster. There is no guarantee that a sick person will become whole if we pray for his or her recovery from illness. At the same time there has never been a dearth of charlatans who play upon the gullibility of the people and claim to work miracles with their prayers and spiritual powers. During the lifetime of Guru Nanak, Babur, the king of Afghanistan, invaded India. Guru Nanak was surprised to find that instead of concentrating on strong defensive measures, the people gathered in holy places to pray for the intervention of divine power to halt the advance of the invader. The following hymn of Guru Nanak's describes the consequences of such lopsided thinking and such a false notion of prayer:

> When they heard the Emperor coming, countless holy men by their prayers offered to thwart his plans and check his progress. Babur came all the same, and burnt houses, mansions, palaces and all. He cut princes into pieces and had them rolled in dust. The holy men worked no miracles though they said they would. No Mughal was rendered blind.
>
> Adi Granth 417

The Purpose of Prayer

The purpose of prayer is not to escape from the harsh realities of everyday life, but to nerve us for a life of effort and sacrifice. It focuses our attention on the problem. When we pray for others, our hearts flow out in sympathy for them and lead us to appreciate their needs better. If it fails to move us to help them overcome their sufferings, it means that we were not sincere and our prayer for them was just lip-service.

Wealth and prosperity, learning and fame, do not necessarily bring peace and contentment. Spiritual discipline and self-control are the true occupation of the mind. These come from the pursuit of truth without worldly attachments and selfishness. The aim of prayer should therefore be to discipline the emotions, to obey God in all circumstances and to live in truth. This can be achieved only through meditation. Guru Nanak has stressed the importance of this aspect of prayer: 'Nanak has only this prayer to offer, if such be your will, O Lord. Bless me that I may be attuned to your name and ever sing your praises' (Adi Granth 752/4).

A Prayer

The whole of the Guru Granth Sahib consists of devotional songs and prayers. Here is one that is often sung in the *gurdwara*:

> O God, I lean on you for you are always with me.
> Be merciful, O, my Lord, that I contemplate ever your name filled with your love.
> I have no other support.
> I accept whatever you do or cause to be done.
> You are my honour. Your nearness is my deliverance, your virtuous words my riches.
> O, God, Nanak seeks the refuge of your feet for this is what he has learnt from holy men.

Adi Granth 677: Guru Arjan

1 What is prayer?
2 Write out and learn the prayer that a Sikh may offer before eating a meal or beginning a journey or some other activity.
3 Discuss why Sikhs say that intention is what matters most in praying.
4 If there is no point in asking God for material things or even recovery from illness, is there any sense in a Sikh's praying? You may find the passages from the Guru Granth Sahib given in the text helpful in your discussions.

MEDITATION

Meditation is a method for attempting to concentrate the mind and thoughts on God. For Sikhs this is *nam simran*. All Sikhs are encouraged to get up early in the morning and take a bath if their health and the weather permit, or at least wash their faces, hands and feet to clear away drowsiness, before sitting for meditation. 'After taking a bath, meditate on your Lord, and your body and mind become pure' (Adi Granth 611: Guru Arjan).

In India people take a bath almost every day as a matter of habit, whether they say prayers afterwards or not. Most of the large *gurdwaras* have large, artificial pools of water attached to them for pilgrims to take a bath in if they wish. These are called *sarowars*, the reservoirs of sacred water. The meaning of bathing in such pools is spiritual. Pilgrims will already have bathed at home!

The Purpose of Meditation

Instincts and desires embedded deep in the mind play a very important part in the formation of our characters. Constant hammering of the subconscious with the remembrance of God therefore paves the way for a life of spiritual peace. The mind which is fixed on God becomes godly; that which concentrates on evil becomes evil.

Bathing in a sarowar
outside a gurdwara *in
Delhi.*

'Man becomes like the one he serves' said Guru Nanak (Adi Granth
224). *Simran*, or remembrance of the holy name, is not a mechanical
repetition of a syllable, phrase or religious text, but a reflection and
concentration on the nature of God. By reflecting on the concept
'God is truth', for example, one is reminded to practise truthfulness
in thought, word and deed. If God is kind, so we must practise charity
and social service; and so on. *Nam simran* cannot, therefore, be
relegated to a once-a-week activity reserved for a special day
only:

> In the ambrosial hours of the dawn repeat the true name and meditate on
> his greatness.
>
> Adi Granth 2: Guru Nanak

> Meditating on the Lord cleans the scum of your mind.
>
> Adi Granth 284: Guru Arjan

> If one remains absorbed in the True One, one's life becomes truthful. To
> meditate on the word of God is the most virtuous act.
>
> Adi Granth 158/2: Guru Amar Das

The Form of Meditation

Devotees will wrap round themselves a blanket, a woollen shawl or a
cotton sheet, close their eyes to help shut their minds to visible
distractions, and repeat '*Waheguru, waheguru*' (wonderful Lord) for
as long as they can. After that, they will recite the special text for the
morning service called *Japji Sahib*. Many Sikhs know *Japji Sahib* by
heart and they will recite it while getting ready for work before
breakfast, or will meditate on it while doing the household chores.
Some will read it from the prayer books called *gutkas*. Many families
these days listen to it recorded on cassettes. Men and women who
have free time during the day visit the *gurdwaras* or read the
scriptures at home. There are set prayers for the evening and
bedtime as well.

This ritual constitutes the *nitname*, the daily prayer programme of
an initiated Sikh. Many Sikhs who cannot perform the full *nitname*

still try to do as much as they can to meet this religious obligation according to the time and opportunities available to them.

When to Meditate or Pray

In the highly industrialised society of today, with its round-the-clock work, keeping to the old schedules made when life was simpler and more leisurely is quite difficult. Prayer demands time and concentration. Sikh prayer can be made at any time, may be performed standing, kneeling or sitting, and facing in any direction. A Sikh is therefore free to pray at any time of the day when the opportunity presents itself: 'True and acceptable is the time when one recognises the Lord's name' (Adi Granth 422/6), and 'Those engaging in devotion do not wait to enquire the auspicious hour' (Adi Granth 35/4).

A Sikh is not always required to stop work for the sake of prayer or meditation. Both can go together. Peasants can utter *'Waheguru, waheguru'* while oiling the wheels of a cart of driving a pair of oxen to the fields. Masons can lay bricks while remembering God with their tongues; and though it may not be possible for authors or reporters to concentrate on their work while praying, the presence of God could be felt in the subconscious.

The Place of Set Prayers

Not everybody is competent to gather stray and scattered thoughts into a directed coherent whole. A set form of prayer or a song of praise help people to fix their minds on God. But for a realised soul or a saint there is no need to depend on any external authority in the form of a scripture or a manual of prayers. His or her wisdom is obvious to everyone.

The following verse sums up Sikh teaching on prayer and meditation:

One who is called a disciple of the Guru should rise early in the morning and contemplate the Lord's name; dwell upon the Lord through the Guru's word so that all sins are washed away; with the sunrise should sing the hymns of praise composed by the Guru; and should remember the name while performing daily chores. The person who repeats the name with every breath is a dear disciple of the Guru.

Adi Granth 305–6: Guru Ram Das

---

1   What is meditation? Do there seem to be any differences between prayer and meditation in Sikhism? If so, what are they?
2   **a** Explain the term that Sikhs use for 'meditation'.
     b What different ways of meditating do Sikhs use?
3   Memorise the advice given by Guru Ram Das (Adi Granth 305–6). Why do you think he encouraged Sikhs to pray or meditate first thing in the morning, even before sunrise?

Chapter 14

Food, Drink and Fasting

FOOD

'Friend, avoid that food which harms the body or provokes evil thoughts', said Guru Nanak (Adi Granth 16). For many Indians that will mean being vegetarian because, they believe, meat results in things like bad temper, high blood pressure and cancers. The body should be kept pure, and meat defiles it, they feel. Many Sikhs are vegetarian for this kind of reason, but the Gurus did not require it of their followers. Once Guru Nanak said, 'Only fools wrangle about eating or not eating meat. They don't know what is flesh, what is vegetable, or what is evil' (Adi Granth 1,289). What concerned him was moral impurity. Being non-vegetarian or vegetarian could not protect anyone from that. A God-centred life was the only guarantee of such purity.

Common sense and hygiene should determine a Sikh's diet, so in the heat of summer in India it might be wise to avoid meat, whereas in winter in Europe or America it might not matter so much. The staple diet of the Punjab in northern India, where most Sikhs still live, is vegetables, pulses (*dahl*) and bread in the form of chappatis (wheat- or maize-flour pancakes). Milk puddings are popular and hot milk is often drunk before going to bed. Clarified butter (*ghee*) is used for cooking, rather than lard or cooking oil. If meat is eaten it is usually only on special occasions such as festivals. It is too expensive to be part of the daily diet.

Forbidden Meat

One kind of meat is forbidden; not that of any particular animal but that which has been prepared in a certain way. Sikhs should not eat *halal* meat – that is, meat from animals slaughtered according to Muslim religious teaching and rites. In the Mughal period the rulers insisted that non-Muslims too should eat only meat prepared in that way. The method called *jhatka*, cutting the neck of the animal with one stroke of the sword or axe, was not allowed. When Sikhs began to assert their independence in the late seventeenth and eighteenth centuries, they reacted against the practices and laws of their rulers. They were not allowed to ride horses or carry weapons, so they did; and they also rejected the *halal* rule. This was one of Guru Gobind Singh's commands to the Khalsa when he formed them at the Baisakhi gathering of 1699.

84

Food in *Gurdwaras*

Outside India, many Sikhs still choose to eat Punjabi food, just as many Britons living in India eat British dishes. However, many young Sikhs have acquired a taste for fish and chips, burgers and pizzas, and other fast foods. Not surprisingly, though, *gurdwaras* maintain the Punjabi traditions. They also serve only vegetarian food so that no members of the community or visitors will be offended or embarrassed. Everyone who goes to the *gurdwara* is expected to share in the communal meal, *langar*. It is a way of sharing in the Sikh belief in the equality of all human beings, as well as accepting typical Indian hospitality. Outside India this meal is usually taken after the service, but at festivals and in India food is served continuously throughout the day in the *gurdwaras* of large towns.

Karah prashad is also served to worshippers, but in the place where the service is held, not in another room or out in the open as *langar* may be. It is really an Indian pudding. It is made of equal parts of plain flour (or semolina), clarified butter and sugar.

Langar *in Britain.*

Langar *in India.*

1   What is the difference between ritual impurity and moral impurity? Which did the Gurus think mattered?
2   Why did Guru Gobind Singh forbid the eating of *halal* meat?
3   Why might many Sikhs prefer to eat Punjabi food even though they are now living in America or Europe?
4   How do Sikhs use food to show that they are members of one family?
5   How do they show their concern for family unity at *langar*?

DRINK   Intoxicants

Intoxicants in any form and drugs of all kinds, including alcohol and tobacco, are strictly forbidden to Sikhs. Once a group of holy men told Guru Nanak that their use of drugs helped them in their meditation. He said he doubted whether their piety was genuine. His own view was that such things enfeebled the brain, weakened the body and made the user unfit to serve society. He also said: 'It makes one crazy and senseless and often leads to wickedness' (Adi Granth 553). Intoxicants such as alcohol or drugs should also be unnecessary for someone who knows God: 'Why should one who deals in the nectar of God's name develop love for mere wine?' (Adi Granth 360).

The Code of Discipline

The Sikh Code of Discipline, the 'Rahit Maryada', forbids the use of drugs and alcohol, and Sikhs who break this rule should not be allowed to sit on the management committees of *gurdwaras*. They may also be excluded from the *sangat* until they agree to mend their ways, accept a penance and then be reinstated. This penance might be cleaning the shoes of the congregation – a degrading act as a punishment, but one which otherwise a Sikh might be eager to do as a form of community service – or cleaning the *gurdwara*. The *Gurdwara* Act of 1925 and the Delhi *Gurdwara* Act of 1971 state that Sikhs who drink or use drugs cannot even be on the electoral role of a *gurdwara*. Visitors to *gurdwaras* should never take alcohol or tobacco with them and preferably should not have traces of them upon their breath.

It is customary in British society to give bottles of wine or spirits as a present. Sikhs should neither give them nor receive them. When the Mughal Emperor Babur invited Guru Nanak to accept a gift of *bhang* (cannabis), he was told: 'God's fear is my *bhang*, my mind is the container, and my intoxication is through this "drug"' (Adi Granth 721).

What reasons might a Sikh give for:
a not smoking?
b not drinking alcohol?
Do they differ from reasons which are generally given for avoiding smoking and alcohol?

FASTING

Sikhism does not regard fasting or either eating or abstaining from certain foods as the way to holiness or spiritual freedom. The Guru Granth Sahib strongly denounces an extreme type of asceticism involving fasting over a prolonged period of time, either to curb passions or to acquire occult powers, as practised by some yogic cults. A healthy human body is considered essential for work, prayer and serving fellow human beings. Complete or partial abstinence from food on a fixed day of the week or month does not bring the soul nearer to God. Repentance is possible without fasting, and keeping God in mind is the way to holiness: 'By practising stubborn self-torture, the body wears out. Through fasting and penance the soul is not softened. Nothing else equals the remembrance of God' (Adi Granth 905/4).

Why is fasting not important to Sikhs?

<table>
<tr><td>

Chapter

15

</td><td>

The Status of Women

</td></tr>
</table>

In many societies women have traditionally been considered as inferior beings and denied independent thinking and status. Until recently, higher education was not considered suitable for them. In Western society, women have been able to improve their position a great deal, but they have not met with the same success in the area of religion. In the East, the situation is much the same.

The Sikh religion, however, gives women a position of equality with men in both secular and religious areas of life. In the teachings of the Sikh Gurus, men and women are equal in the sight of God. They share equally the grace of God and are individually accountable for their actions to God. The different roles a person may fulfil in society are not allowed to reflect on one's human dignity, whether one is male or female.

SOCIAL ROLES

Traditionally, men were the breadwinners, and it was left to them to devise ways and means to provide the necessities of life. Women generally did not interfere with their work, but felt that it was their duty to run the home and bring up children. Women still take pride in this work, which is equally important to the welfare of home and community.

The Gurus' Teachings

Guru Nanak highlighted the social importance of women by appreciating their role in the preservation of society, in the proper development of the family, as wives and mothers, and in cementing the social ties and relationships. 'Man builds the house; it is woman who turns it into a home' is an old Punjabi saying. Guru Nanak asked why women should be regarded as insignificant and unimportant when 'It is from women that we are conceived and born. Woman is our life-long friend and keeps the race going. Why should we despise her who gives birth to great men?' (Adi Granth 473).

Guru Nanak exalted the status of women by idealising the love of a wife for her husband and holding it up as an example for a devotee of God:

> My beloved Lord is not distant. When my soul was reconciled to the word of the Guru, I found God the prop of my life. In this way the bride met God, the bridegroom, and became his beloved.
>
> Adi Granth 1,197

A woman in Sikhism is considered as a man's helpmate and as indispensable for his spiritual growth and morality. The householder's life is therefore considered to be the normal and the natural way of existence. The Sikh viewpoint cannot be better stressed than in the following assertion of a seventeenth-century Sikh theologian: 'From a temporal as well as spiritual point of view woman is man's other half and assists him to salvation' (Bhai Gurdas: Var 5/16).

THE HUSBAND/ WIFE RELATIONSHIP

In so far as marital fidelity is concerned, no distinction is made between husband and wife. There should be no double standards of chastity among Sikhs. The keeping of marriage vows is demanded of both the parties to the marriage.

Guru Amar Das ordained:

> Widowed is that bride who robed in the red bridal trousseau goes out to enjoy the bed of one other than her lord. Thus she deserts her own home enticed by the love of another. It tastes sweet to her but her enjoyment leads to pain.
>
> Adi Granth 785

And 'What happiness can there be for one without virtue, O lady?' asked Guru Nanak (Adi Granth 56).

The husband is also warned 'Do not cast your eyes on the beauty of another's wife' (Adi Granth 274). He should rather 'regard beautiful women who are the partners of others as his mothers, sisters and daughters' (Bhai Gurdas: Var 26/11).

The concept of the husband/wife relationship is considered as very special. Husband and wife are therefore enjoined to work for a complete identification of interests to make a success of married life. 'They are not man and wife who have physical contact only. Only they are truly wedded who have one spirit in two bodies' (Adi Granth 788: Guru Amar Das).

Widows and Divorcees

The inhuman custom of *sati* (the burning to death of widows on their husbands' pyre) was common throughout the medieval period of Indian history and right up to the time of the British conquering of India. Only in the nineteenth century was this cruel practice declared illegal, and prevented by the government. (High-caste Hindus did not approve the remarriage of their widows, though a widower could have a second marriage soon after the death of his first wife.)

The Sikh Gurus strongly condemned the treatment meted out to widows for no fault of their own, and pleaded for allowing them to lead a normal happy life, saying that 'Widows who lead a life of contentment and chastity deserve to be respected' (Adi Granth 787: Guru Amar Das). The killing of female babies (female infanticide), also practised in India at the time, was strongly denounced by the Gurus too. Their tough attitude to and strong stand against these social evils prevented their seeping into the build-up of the Sikh community. No stigma is attached to the remarriage of a widow or a divorcee among the Sikhs. The marriage will take place in the normal way, as described in Chapter 4.

ROLES IN RELIGIOUS WORSHIP

The Sikh religion does not discriminate against women concerning the reading of scriptures at home or in the *gurdwara* (see Chapter 11). Any Sikh man or woman may conduct ceremonies, sing hymns, or speak in the *gurdwara*. Within 20 years of the death of Guru Nanak, Guru Amar Das – the third Guru – extended the right of preaching to women and appointed worthy women to act as missionaries, along with men.

A woman reading from the Guru Granth Sahib in a gurdwara.

Women singing kirtan *in one of their gatherings for worship.*

The household chores in Indian village homes, with very few modern facilities for washing and cooking, keep women so fully occupied that it becomes virtually impossible for them to become involved in the social and religious affairs of the community. As a result, most Sikh congregations in India are dominated by men. In England, however, women often serve on the management committees of *gurdwaras*. Women presidents and secretaries are to be found in a number of them.

SUMMARY

In the end it must be said that though man and woman are regarded as equal in the sight of God, in social life the woman is certainly given a subordinate role to play. The Sikh marriage service includes all the rites of the time when a women was under a man's guardianship, and the way in which the service is conducted leads one to the inevitable conclusion of the inferiority of women. There is small consolation in saying that Sikh brides do not wear a veil at their wedding and that they retain their maiden names after marriage. Outside India they do add the surnames of their husbands to their given names in conformity to Western customs. Simply to use the Sikh name 'Kaur' is difficult.

1   What do you think Sikh women in Britain will have to do in order to win the equality which the Gurus preached about?
2   Why is it difficult for Sikhs simply to use the names 'Kaur' or 'Singh' in a country such as Britain?

Chapter 16	# *Worship, Work and Helping the Needy*

Sikh ethics can be summed up in three clear-cut phrases: pray as much as you can, work as much as you can, and give as much as you can.

PRAY AS MUCH AS YOU CAN

The primary human duty is to God and is expressed through daily worship and occasional feasts and festivals. The Sikh emphasis on the purposeful reading of the religious texts is meant to keep God in the forefront of life. 'Why waver, O man, when your creator will certainly keep you? So meditate on your Lord as long as you have breath' said Guru Arjan (Adi Granth 724/6).

WORK AS MUCH AS YOU CAN

Work is a social necessity. You cannot get everything for the asking. To have a comfortable life and to pray in peace and dignity people have to work to earn a living. Every ablebodied person has therefore a moral duty to do some useful work for society. It is not permitted to a Sikh to beg and live off the earnings of others: 'He alone has found the right way who eats what he earns through toil and shares his earnings with the needy' (Adi Granth 1,245).

There is no place for social parasites in Sikhism. People cannot absolve themselves from labour, on the pretext of devoting their time to worship and contemplation, in view of such strong warnings in the

Giving water to pilgrims outside the Golden Temple in Amritsar.

Families sitting on the causeway (parkarma) at the Golden Temple before returning home.

Sikh scripture as these: 'Is it not shameful that a holy man should beg from door to door?' (Adi Granth 903), and 'Cursed is the life of those who trade in the name of God' (Adi Granth 1,245/1) – that is, those who make money from being 'religious professionals'.

Status and Wealth

It does not matter, however, what form of work – manual, skilled, professional, trade or agricultural – one is engaged in, as long as it does not involve deceit, double-dealing or other underhand ways. No loss of status is involved in doing manual or menial work. Disgrace and humiliation come from immoral and illegal transactions, from supporting and propagating the production of harmful intoxicants and drugs, and from promoting pornography and prostitution.

Work is essential to provide for the basic needs of food, clothing, shelter and helping the needy, but the pursuit of wealth as an end in itself and using it as a status symbol are fraught with dangers and difficulties. 'He who has more is worn by care. He who has less wanders about in search of more. He alone is in peace who has neither too much or too little' said Guru Arjan (Adi Granth 1,019).

Creating wealth by legitimate and morally approved methods and working for all-round prosperity are commendable. The love of money for its own sake, however, and acquiring it by oppressing those whose poverty makes them defenceless, and by depriving others of their due by ingenious tricks, is denounced by Guru Nanak. He says, 'It is said that if clothes are stained with blood, the garment is polluted. If that is so, what of the blood-sucker? How can his mind be pure?' (Adi Granth 140).

Young Sikhs presenting a cheque to a charity after raising the money through sponsored activities.

1   What is a 'social parasite'?
2   Why is there no place for such people in Sikhism?

GIVE AS MUCH AS YOU CAN

'Give as much as you can' does not mean that you should give only a portion of your surplus wealth to help those who deserve attention. It means that you might have to forego or cut down your own needs to meet the bare necessities of a fellow human being. It calls for a sacrifice on your part. We must remember that 'God's bounty belongs to all, but in this world it is not shared justly' (Adi Granth 1,171). So what has been given in common for the use of all must not be taken by the few. (See Chapter 17 too.) 'If we want to get a seat in the court of God, we should dedicate ourselves in this world to the service of the people' declared Guru Nanak (Adi Granth 26).

Daswandh

Guru Amar Das introduced the idea that Sikhs should give a tenth of their surplus wealth to the service of the community. This is called *daswandh*. The money given is used for such things as building schools and hospitals or famine relief. *Gurdwaras* do not have a system for assessing contributions such as governments use to collect taxes. What Sikhs give is a matter for their own consciences.

1   *'Nam japna, kirt karna, vand chakna'* – 'pray as much as you can, work as much as you can, and give as much as you can'. Why do you think Sikhs consider the three to be inseparable?
2   Divide a page in your notebook or file in two. Put the heading 'Acceptable job' at the top of one column and 'Unacceptable job' at the top of the other. Put the following occupations into the section where you think Sikhs would put them, and under each give one or more reasons for your decision.

nurse   beggar
priest   shop keeper
road sweeper   carpenter
prostitute   car mechanic
pub owner   market trader

Equality and Justice

'*Ek pita ekas ke ham barak*' (We are all children of one and the same father, Almighty God) (Adi Granth 611/18). The idea put forward by Sikhism is not new. What is new is the emphasis placed upon it.

HISTORICAL ORIGINS

At the time when Sikhism was founded, Hindus accepted the caste system (see below) and so rejected the concept of social and religious equality altogether. Islam extended complete social equality to its followers, but not to non-Muslims. Sikhism in its infancy and growth had to steer clear of the two diametrically opposed systems of beliefs and practices prevailing in India, Hinduism and Islam. Guru Nanak did this by means of the institutions of *sangat* (worshipping together) and *pangat* (dining together). Through these he tried to end the religion-backed, birth-based system of segregation and to make social integration a part of the Sikh path. Religious intolerance and political discrimination, practised by many Muslim rulers of the time against their many non-Muslim subjects, threatened national unity.

Guru Nanak was an eye-witness to Babur's invasion in 1526 and to the terrible sufferings people had to undergo. Both Hindu and Muslim communities suffered equal humiliation. Guru Nanak writes that: 'Some lost their five times of prayer and of some the time of worship is gone. Without sacred squares [private areas for bathing and cooking] how shall the Hindu women now bathe and apply frontal marks?' (Adi Granth 417), and that 'The wives of the Hindus, of Muslims and of the Rajput brave have had their raiments torn from head to foot. They go now wandering madly about amongst their dead' (Adi Granth 418).

Guru Nanak called the emperor a tyrant, an evil genius who had brought about havoc with his army. At the complaint of the Guru, the emperor ordered the release of people taken as prisoners and returned the property that had been looted by his soldiers. Guru Nanak then blessed the king, saying that 'A king remains installed on the throne by virtue of his good qualities alone' (Adi Granth 992).

THE CASTE SYSTEM

From time immemorial to the conquering of India by the Muslims, the religious practices, economic activities and criminal and civil laws reflected the basic assumptions and inequalities of the caste system. Put simply, this system is like a ladder with four rungs, with Brahmins (the priestly class) at the top, Shudras (the servant class) at the bottom, and Kshatriyas (ruler-warriors) and Vaishyas (merchants and farmers) forming its middle rungs. The members of each caste group (*jati*) are born into the same occupation or range of occupations. For example, *ramgarhias* are traditionally carpenters, masons and blacksmiths. Not many now follow the old occupations, but people still usually marry other members of the same *jati*.

People born into groups outside the caste system are thought to pollute members of these castes if they touch them or are near them. These 'outcastes' were known as 'untouchables' until this century, but are now called scheduled classes or exterior castes. Article 15 of the Constitution of India prohibits discrimination on the grounds of religion, race, caste and sex.

Guru Nanak and his successors questioned the very basis of the caste system, and said that: 'We [all human beings] are God's own people, neither high nor low nor in between' (Adi Granth 504), and that 'God does not mind our caste or birth. So let us learn the way of truthful living, for one's deeds proclaim one's caste and respect' (Adi Granth 1,330). Some so-called untouchables who have become Sikhs are members of the highest religious institutions of Sikhism.

How would you react to being asked to look after the shoes at a gurdwara? Can you think of reasons why some Sikhs consider this to be a great honour?

Guru Nanak and his immediate successors came from the Hindu fold and as a consequence early Sikh congregations always consisted of Hindu converts and sympathisers. At no stage of Sikhism's development did Muslims join in any large numbers. Every care was therefore taken to keep the movement immune from the evils of the caste system. Nevertheless, the ideal, casteless Sikh community has still to be achieved.

EQUALITY IN PRACTICE

Sikhs were equally opposed to the discriminatory taxes imposed by the Muslim rulers in the seventeenth century on the non-Muslim population of their territories. The religious oppression let loose by them turned the Sikhs into saint-soldiers. In the first half of the nineteenth century the Sikhs were able to establish a kingdom of their own in the north-west of India.

Under Maharaja Ranjit Singh they had the opportunity to put Sikh principles to the test. The maharaja stood by the Gurus' teachings and acted upon them. 'Religion consists not in mere talk. He who looks on all alike and considers all as equal is acclaimed as truly religious' (Adi Granth 730). That is what he did. His foreign and home ministers were Muslim and his treasury officials were Hindus. Money was given to build and support mosques and *mandirs* (Muslim and Hindu places of worship) as well as the Golden Temple, the centre of Sikh worship in Amritsar. (See Chapter 10 for the origins of the Golden Temple.)

1   **a** What do *sangat* and *pangat* mean?
    b Explain why Sikhs regard each of them as very important.
2   Why is the Sikh ideal one of equality for all?
3   What reasons can you suggest to explain why the ideal has never become a complete reality?

Chapter

18

Sikhism Today

More than 500 years after the birth of Guru Nanak in 1469, Sikhs are to be found in many countries. Most of them – about 12 million – live in the State of Punjab in northern India. Outside the Punjab, Delhi has a Sikh population approaching half a million and there are many Sikhs in Calcutta, Bombay and other major Indian cities.

ENGLISH-SPEAKING COUNTRIES

Sikhs have also migrated to other Commonwealth and English-speaking countries because of their historical links with the British Empire and their readiness to go wherever opportunity for economic improvement presents itself.

In the 1890s, Sikhs and other Indians went to Africa to help the British develop their new colonies. When Kenya, Uganda and other countries became independent some Asians left them to make a new life in Britain or America. Those in Uganda were expelled in 1972 and became refugees. The reason why many Asians came to Britain rather than going to India was that their links, through the Empire and Commonwealth, were greater with the British than with the country which their parents or grandparents had left. They also realised that India was overpopulated and presented few opportunities compared with other countries.

Britain has more Sikhs than any other part of the world outside India, perhaps 400,000, but Canada and the USA may have nearly 200,000 between them, and there are others in Australia, New Zealand, Singapore, Hong Kong and Fiji. Small numbers have gone to such other countries as Norway, Denmark and Germany. Sikhs continue to look for opportunities outside India. Many now work in Dubai and other Gulf states, but their families remain in India. There may be between one and two million Sikhs now living outside India but no one knows the exact numbers.

1 Why do people leave the land of their birth to settle elsewhere?
2 What made Sikhs from India come to Britain rather than to other European countries in the 1950s?
3   a Why did Sikhs and other people of Asian origin leave Uganda in 1972?

    b What reasons had they for leaving other African countries at that time?

American Sikhs

In the USA a Sikh, Har Bhajan Singh Yogi, taught meditation in the 1960s and encouraged those who came to his classes to adopt healthy eating habits (vegetarianism) and disciplined lives, including the rejection of drugs, smoking, alcohol and sex outside marriage. A number of these men and women converted to the Sikh faith. They can be recognised by their Indian clothing, always white, and the turban which both men and women wear. They live in communities called *ashrams*. Some of their children go to Sikh schools in India. These American Sikhs have a special devotion to the hymns of Guru Ram Das.

Americans who have become Sikhs dress in white from head to foot. Women as well as men wear turbans.

Changes

Changes are bound to occur when people leave their own country. A main one for Sikhs has been the use of the weekend for festive celebrations and worship. In India, *gurdwaras* are usually open every day. British, Canadian or Australian *gurdwaras* may only open on Sundays. Weddings which in India take place in the open air, often under a marquee, are solemnised elsewhere in *gurdwaras*.

Although Sikhs reject caste they have never succeeded in shaking it off completely, any more than the Indian Christians have. Members of different caste groups may live in separate villages in the Punjab and not mix very much. Intermarriage (marriage between people from different castes) is not normal. Abroad – in Britain, for example – Sikhs of different groups are finding themselves living in the same street, working in the same factory. Very often they mix happily in the *gurdwara*, but not always. Some groups may stress the turban and keeping the five Ks, others may consider shaving acceptable and not be very particular about the turban. Some may drink alcohol and eat meat, others may be very strictly against smoking and be vegetarian. Tensions can arise and do. It can be hard for someone whose family has always kept the uncut hair and turban to mix with a Sikh who covers his short hair with a handkerchief when he goes to the *gurdwara* and makes a living as a tobacconist. For these kinds of reason, separate *gurdwaras* have sometimes emerged where different groups – *bhattras, jats* or *ramgarhias* – control the committee.

These three groups have different occupational backgrounds. *Bhattras* were traders and first came to Britain to work in market stalls and sell goods door-to-door. *Jats* are farmers in the Punjab and *ramgarhias* are carpenters, joiners, blacksmiths and craftworkers of all kinds. Many of them took their skills to East Africa. In the countries where they have settled, as in India, the groups now work in all kinds of jobs, as doctors, lawyers, teachers, shopkeepers, nurses or accountants, but they still tend to marry among their own group and keep their own traditions. (See Chapter 17.) It must be remembered, however, that they are all Sikhs. At critical moments differences are set aside in the interests of unity, as when, for example, there is racial tension and Sikhs feel threatened.

?

1 After a class discussion, list reasons why:
   a someone might convert to Sikhism as some Americans have.
   b a Sikh might convert to some other religion, as some have.
   c some aspects of Sikhism might present difficulties for potential converts. Which aspects are these?
2 What changes in religious practices have occurred among British Sikhs? Why have they been necessary?
3 Why might two groups of Sikhs decide to set up separate *gurdwaras*?
4 What issues would unite them in common action?

SIKH MOVEMENTS

If you had been able to visit the Punjab about 150 years ago you might have found very few Sikhs wearing the five Ks. In *gurdwaras* you might have found statues of Hindu gods, and Hindu priests reading the Guru Granth Sahib. In their struggle to survive during the persecutions of the eighteenth century, Sikhs had let *gurdwaras* pass into the care of Hindus. Those Sikhs who were not involved in the armed struggle may have given up their distinctive appearance to look like Hindus when Afghan or Mughal soldiers came to their villages to take them away. Sikhs had a price on their heads.

In 1799 a young Sikh general, Maharaja Ranjit Singh, who was only 19 at the time, captured Lahore, the largest city of the Punjab. He established an independent state which lasted until 1849, when the British added it to their empire. During his reign and ever since, Sikhs have been free to practise their religion, but the old ways did not change overnight.

Sikhism as we know it today owes much to three movements, the Nirankaris, the Namdharis, and the Singh Sabha movement.

The Nirankaris

The Nirankaris were inspired by a man called Dayal Das, who died in 1855. Many years earlier, as a young man, he was shocked to discover that Sikhs were being married according to Hindu rites by Brahmin priests, with the Guru Granth Sahib nowhere in sight. He began to bring back the practices of basing naming and marriage ceremonies upon the Guru Granth Sahib.

Dayal Das was a deeply spiritual man who was more interested in the devotional aspects of Sikhism than the Khalsa ideal. He made something of a distinction between the two. He described Guru Nanak as 'Nanak *nirankar*', the formless one. The name '*nirankar*' was sometimes used by Guru Nanak to describe God (see Chapter 12).

Much of what the Nirankaris wanted became possible with the passing of the *Anand* Marriage Act of 1909 and the *Gurdwara* Act of 1925. These gave Sikhs both the legal right to conduct their own form of wedding ceremonies and also control of the *gurdwaras*.

The Namdharis

Another leader of resistance to the lax practices which had entered Sikhism was Baba Ram Singh (1816–85). He found Sikhs taking drugs, drinking alcohol and eating meat. Instead of simple wedding ceremonies, marriages were extravagant and the groom's parents demanded costly dowries, completely against Sikh principles. Baba Ram Singh even went so far as to remind Sikhs that the Gurus had permitted the remarriage of widows. He also encouraged mixed, intercaste marriages.

Some of his followers took part in agitation which resulted in riots. Sixty-six of these followers were executed by the British, who tied them across the muzzles of guns which were then fired. Baba Ram Singh, as leader, was exiled to Rangoon in Burma in 1872.

Movements, once begun, tend to continue to exist. Nirankaris and Namdharis have never been great in numbers but they can still be found today.

The Singh Sabha Movement

The pioneering work of Dayal Das and Baba Ram Singh prepared the ground for a more organised and less individualistic response to the challenge of the times, the Singh Sabha movement. The challenge now, however, came not from the dominant Hindu culture to which Sikhs were closely kin. In fact, at the time *jati*, the occupational group to which someone belonged under the Hindu caste system (see Chapter 17), often mattered more than religion. *Jat* (farmer) married *jat* regardless of whether they were Sikh or Hindu, rather than marry a *ramgarhia* (craftworker) of the same religion.

The new threat was from Christian missionaries. In 1834 the Ludhiana Mission was set up by Americans. After 1849, when the Punjab became part of the British Empire, more missionaries started to work in it. Although the number of converts was never great, for a minority religion, threatened until recently by the Mughals, this new danger was very real. The missionaries tended to target the better-off urban Punjabis and to use education as their way of reaching out to young Sikhs, as well as providing literature on Christian subjects. The Sikhs replied by setting up *singh sabhas* (Sikh associations) in some towns, whose aim was to educate Sikhs in their faith.

The situation was made worse in 1877. In that year a Hindu, Dayananda Saraswati, who had started a movement called the Arya Samaj, which was intended to counter the Christian missionary threat to Hinduism, came to the Punjab. He began converting Muslims and Sikhs as well as organising a Hindu revival. This made the Sikhs more energetic. *Sabhas* were formed in most towns. Schools and colleges were set up. Sikh practices were reformed so that, for example, *anand* marriage in the presence of the Guru Granth Sahib replaced weddings conducted by a Hindu priest. In *gurdwaras*, Brahmins gave way to Sikh *granthis*. *Amrit* initiation was revived, and more Sikhs took to wearing the turban and the five Ks, which many had not bothered to do in the past.

It was only in 1909 that Sikhs won the legal right to perform their marriages (the *Anand* Marriage Act) and not until 1925 was their control of *gurdwaras* secure. However, after a generation of agitation their efforts did meet with success. The Sikh religious practices and sense of identity experienced today are the result.

1 What contribution did:
    a Nirankaris
    b Namdharis
    make to the revival of Sikhism?
2 **a** What threats made Sikhs set up *singh sabhas*?
    b How did the Singh Sabha movement counter the threats?

THE PRESENT

The story of all living religions is one of on-going development. As Sikhs have settled outside India they have taken their beliefs and life-styles with them, enhancing the countries in which they have settled. In most respects they are able to adapt to their new environment, learning the language, finding work, establishing careers, worshipping on Sundays in Britain or when they are free from having to earn their living. Sometimes there are cultural clashes. These are usually few, but important.

Cultural Differences

The best-known issue in Britain has been that of the turban. Sometimes local transport authorities refused to allow Sikhs working on the buses to wear turbans. In 1976, an Act of Parliament was passed exempting Sikhs from the 1972 Traffic Act requiring motor-cyclists to wear crash helmets. Some years later the House of Lords ruled in favour of a Sikh boy's right to wear a turban instead of a cap as part of the school uniform. Health and Safety regulations on building sites make it obligatory for employees to wear hard-hats. Sikhs would like to be able to wear turbans instead.

There has been some question whether legislation on offensive weapons would threaten the Sikh religious duty to wear a *kirpan*, but the Home Office has assured Sikhs that it would be exempt, as would be the Scot's dirk.

Although it seldom becomes headline news, the main anxiety of Sikhs in the West today relates to their children. Often they are growing away from the traditions of the Punjab. Preferences for fast-food rather than Indian cuisine may not matter a lot, but their lack of Punjabi makes it difficult for some young Sikhs to share their ideas, hopes or problems with their parents in any serious conversation. It also means they cannot understand many things which are said in the *gurdwara*. Arranged marriages are accepted by many young Sikhs as preferable to the way their friends organise their relationships, especially when parents allow them more say in the choice of a partner, but some no longer regard them to be part of Sikhism. They see arranged marriages as more the life-style of their parents' homeland, not theirs.

The Storming of the Golden Temple

The 1980s were overshadowed by an event which will be remembered by Sikhs as much as the sufferings of earlier centuries. It was the storming of the Golden Temple precincts by the Indian army in June 1984. The Indian government called it Operation Blue Star.

For several years some Sikhs in the Punjab had been asking for greater recognition for their religion and for changes in the province's government which would have amounted to Sikh home rule. The focus of the Sikh cause became a religious teacher, Sant Jarnail Singh Bhindranwale, who eventually made the Golden Temple complex his headquarters. He was accused of organising violent opposition to the government, and of threatening its overthrow. After months of growing tension, the Indian army, led by a Sikh officer, entered the Temple area. In a two-day battle the Sant was killed with most of his followers.

That was not the end of the story. On 31 October 1984, the Indian Prime Minister, Mrs Indira Gandhi, was assassinated by two Sikhs in her bodyguard. Riots broke out in Delhi and other cities. Many Sikhs were killed or injured and their property destroyed, but even five years later none of those responsible for this violence had been named, arrested and charged. In the Punjab, shootings continued to the end of the decade.

A few Sikhs want a separate state of Khalistan, an independent country, 'the land of the pure', to be ruled by Sikhs and centred on the Punjab. There are Sikh cabinet ministers, army officers and civil servants loyal to the Indian government. There are others who oppose the government but also wish to maintain the Republic of India and are against the use of force by Sikh agitators. They do not want the outside world to have a tarnished image of their faith, but they have been scarred by the events of 1984. When they recover, they will be able to continue thinking what it means to be a member of a religion which is to be found worldwide and which is taking its place among the other major religions.

1   Why were Sikhs angered and distressed when they heard that the Indian army had entered the Golden Temple in 1984? Explain your reaction as a Sikh in a letter to a newspaper or in a TV interview.

2   Give the view that a Sikh army officer might have given who took part in Operation Blue Star. You might present this in the form of a letter or TV interview.

3   Why do some Sikhs want to establish an independent Sikh state, Khalistan?

Overview Questions

1   What developments do you think might take place in British Sikhism during the twenty-first century?

2   Now that you have completed a study of this book, though there is much more still to find out about Sikhs and their religion, compile an encyclopaedia article of 500 words entitled 'Sikhism'.

3   If you could read Punjabi and a Sikh gave you a copy of the Guru Granth Sahib, how would you be expected to look after it, and why?

4   Why would Sikhs say 'Whoever believes in God must also believe that life continues beyond death'?

5   Why is pride regarded as a very great evil by Sikhs?

Further Reading

TEACHERS' BOOKS

W. Owen Cole, *Sikhism and its Indian Context* (Darton, Longman and Todd, 1984)
W. Owen Cole, *The Guru in Sikhism* (Darton, Longman and Todd, 1982)
W. Owen Cole and Piara Singh Sambhi, *The Sikhs: Their Religious Beliefs and Practices* (Routledge and Kegan Paul, 1978)
M. A. Macauliffe, *The Sikh Religion* (S. Chand and Co., 1963)
Khushwant Singh, *A History of the Sikhs* (Oxford University Press, 1974)

PUPILS' BOOKS

Davinder Kaur Babraa, *Visiting a Sikh Temple* (Lutterworth, 1981)
W. Owen Cole, *A Sikh Family in Britain* (Religious Education Press, 1973)
W. Owen Cole (ed.), *Comparative Religions* (Blandford, 1982)
W. Owen Cole, *Thinking about Sikhism* (Lutterworth, 1980)
W. Owen Cole with Peggy Morgan, *Six Religions in the Twentieth Century* (Stanley Thornes and Hulton, 1984)
W. Owen Cole and Piara Singh Sambhi, *Baisakhi* (RMEP, 1986)
W. Owen Cole and Piara Singh Sambhi, *Sikhism* (Ward Lock, 1973)
Piara Singh Sambhi, *Understanding Your Sikh Neighbour* (Lutterworth, 1980)
Daljit Singh and Angela Smith, *The Sikh World* (Macdonald, 1985)

Glossary

Adi Granth	The first collection of the Sikh scriptures, compiled by Guru Arjan in 1604; now used to mean the same as Guru Granth Sahib.
Akali	Literally, 'a worshipper of Akal (the Timeless God)': name used for the members of the Akali Dal, a Sikh political party.
Akal Takht	Literally, 'the throne of the Timeless One': name given to the building constructed by Guru Hargobind in 1609, standing opposite the Golden Temple at Amritsar (see Harimandir). All important matters affecting the Sikh community are discussed there and decisions are taken after due deliberation.
Amrit	'The nectar of immortality': a mixture of sugar and water stirred with a *khanda*, blessed by reading over it from the scriptures, and used in the Sikh initiation ceremony. (*Amritpan karna* means 'to take initiation'.)
Anand karaj	Literally, 'ceremony of bliss': name given to a Sikh wedding.
Anand Sahib	Literally, 'song of bliss': a Sikh hymn used at all the ritual services.
Ardas	The formal Sikh communal prayer which is said on all ceremonial occasions.
Baba	Literally, 'grandfather': a term of respect applied to holy men.
Baisakhi	A Sikh festival in April to commemorate the founding of the Khalsa. The name is taken from the month on the first of which the festival is celebrated.
Bani	Revelations of saints and prophets.
Bhai	Literally, 'brother': a title of respect used to describe men of outstanding piety in the Sikh faith.
Channani	The canopy over the Guru Granth Sahib.
Charn-pahul	Literally, 'foot washing': water is poured on the feet of a holy man and caught in a bowl, to be used for the initiation ceremony.
Chauri	Fake hair or nylon fibre fan waved over the Guru Granth Sahib to show respect.
Darbar Sahib	Name used to describe the complex of buildings including the Golden Temple at Amritsar (see Harimandir).
Dasam Granth	Collection of writings attributed to Guru Gobind Singh.
Dharamsala	A building maintained by the Sikh community to be used for religious and social purposes, with rooms for lodging pilgrims and travellers.
Dharma	Religiously and morally approved code of conduct.
Diwali	Autumn Hindu festival of lights associated with the gods Rama and Sita. Sikhs celebrate it in memory of the release of Guru Hargobind from prison.
Diwan	Literally, 'a royal court': name given to an act of Sikh congregational worship.
Gaddi	Seat of a holy man; his headquarters.
Giani	A learned Sikh religious preacher.
Granth	A collection of holy writings.
Granthi	A person entrusted to look after the Guru Granth Sahib and do the reading and ceremonial work in the *gurdwara*.
Gurbani	A Guru's teachings; the contents of the Guru Granth Sahib.
Gurmukh	A God-centred person; a follower of the Guru.
Gurpurb	Anniversary of a Guru's birth or death.

Guru	A spiritual teacher; the term used by Sikhs for their ten historical Gurus, from Guru Nanak to Guru Gobind Singh.
Guru Granth Sahib	The name used for the principal Sikh scripture.
Gutka	A small collection of extracts from the Guru Granth Sahib.
Harimandir	Literally, 'the house of God': the building constructed by Guru Arjan to house the Adi Granth. It is often called the Golden Temple.
Hola Mohalla	Early spring Sikh festival when Sikhs assemble at Anandpur Sahib, in northern India, to display their skill in the use of arms.
Hukam	Literally, 'order': a lesson read from the Guru Granth Sahib.
Janam Sakhi	Collection of stories about the life of Guru Nanak.
Japji	The Sikh morning prayer, a composition of Guru Nanak's.
Jap Sahib	A hymn composed by Guru Gobind Singh. It forms part of the daily prayers of an initiated Sikh.
Jatha	A group of Sikh warriors or protesters; also used for a group of Sikh musicians.
Jivan mukat	Literally, 'liberated soul': used of someone who is liberated spiritually in this life.
Karah prashad	A sweet dish, made with equal portions of flour, sugar and butter, and cooked in an iron bowl. It is served to the congregation at all Sikh ceremonies.
Kaur	Literally, 'the second son of a king', 'princess': name taken by all female Sikhs.
Khalsa	Literally, 'the pure ones': the family of initiated Sikhs, founded in 1699.
Khanda	Double-edged sword; an emblem found on the Sikh flag.
Khande-da amrit	Sikh form of initiation, introduced by Guru Gobind Singh in 1699.
Kirtan	Singing of hymns from the Sikh scriptures to the accompaniment of music.
Langar	Sikh communal meal, served to all free of charge; name given to the dining hall where the free meal is served.
Lavan	Literally, 'to break away from the parental home': name given to the Sikh wedding hymn composed by Guru Ram Das.
Milni	Literally, 'meeting': a formal introduction of the elders of the family before the marriage ceremony.
Namdhari	Literally, 'upholders of the name': a Sikh reform movement started by Baba Ram Singh in the second half of the nineteenth century.
Nam simran	Meditation upon God's name.
Nirankari	Literally, 'worshippers of the Formless God': a Sikh reform movement started by Baba Dayal in the early part of the nineteenth century.
Nishan sahib	Sikh flag flown at the *gurdwara*.
Palki	Wooden structure in which the Guru Granth Sahib is installed in the *gurdwara*.
Panj pyare	Literally, 'the five beloved ones': the original members of the *khalsa*.
Panth	Literally, 'path': used to describe the Sikh community.
Path	Reading of the scriptures.
Sangat	Congregation.
Sant	Holy man.
Sati	Literally, 'a virtuous woman': one who burns herself to death on the funeral pyre of her husband according to Indian tradition.
Singh	Literally, 'lion': name used by all male Sikhs.
Tirath	A Hindu place of pilgrimage.
Var	Literally, 'ballad': name used to describe the compositions of Bhai Gurdas, a Sikh theologian who helped Guru Arjan compile the Guru Granth Sahib.

Index